MEN AND WOMEN:

Partners at Work

George F. Simons & G. Deborah Weissman

A FIFTY-MINUTE™ SERIES BOOK

CRISP PUBLICATIONS, INC.
Menlo Park, California

MEN AND WOMEN:
Partners at Work

George F. Simons & G. Deborah Weissman

CREDITS
Editor: **Michael G. Crisp**
Typesetting: **Interface Studio**
Cover Design: **Carol Harris**
Artwork: **Ralph Mapson**

Copyright © 1990 by Crisp Publications, Inc.
Printed in the United States of America

English language Crisp books are distributed worldwide. Our major international distributors include:

CANADA: Reid Publishing Ltd., Box 69559—109 Thomas St., Oakville, Ontario, Canada L6J 7R4. TEL: (905) 842-4428, FAX: (905) 842-9327

Raincoast Books Distribution Ltd., 112 East 3rd Avenue, Vancouver, British Columbia, Canada V5T 1C8. TEL: (604) 873-6581, FAX: (604) 874-2711

AUSTRALIA: Career Builders, P.O. Box 1051, Springwood, Brisbane, Queensland, Australia 4127. TEL: 841-1061, FAX: 841-1580

NEW ZEALAND: Career Builders, P.O. Box 571, Manurewa, Auckland, New Zealand. TEL: 266-5276, FAX: 266-4152

JAPAN: Phoenix Associates Co., Mizuho Bldg. 2-12-2, Kami Osaki, Shinagawa-Ku, Tokyo 141, Japan. TEL: 3-443-7231, FAX: 3-443-7640

Selected Crisp titles are also available in other languages. Contact International Rights Manager Suzanne Kelly at (415) 323-6100 for more information.

This book is printed on recyclable paper with soy ink.

Library of Congress Catalog Card Number 89-81518
Simons, George F. & Weissman, G. Deborah
Men and Women
ISBN 1-56052-009-4

ABOUT THIS BOOK

MEN AND WOMEN: Partners at Work can be used in a variety of ways, including:

- **As Personal Enrichment.** This book is designed to be an effective self study tool. You will both read and ''do'' from beginning to end. The basic concepts are highlighted by easy-to-understand examples, followed by exercises that you can practice, retain, and use day after day.

- **With a Co-worker.** If you read this book and complete its exercises with a colleague of the other sex, you will benefit immediately by putting into practice what the book teaches. Because the focus is on person-to-person skills, you will be testing and applying what you learn at every step along the way.

- **For Organizational Change.** If this book is distributed throughout an organization, the communication and productivity of women and men working together will improve. Personnel and training departments may use it to support their programs, or create a training seminar from it.

- **In Education.** *Men and Women* can serve as a basic or auxiliary text for high school, university or continuing adult education in psychology, the social sciences or men's and women's studies. Because of its unique blend of theory and practice, students can use it to both investigate the issues and develop useful skills.

ABOUT THE AUTHORS

Dr. George Simons is Principal of George Simons International, a Santa Cruz, CA consulting group whose mission is to enable diverse individuals and groups to work together creatively and productively. He has trained people to work together more effectively in more than 25 countries. Among the clients he has served are Apple Computer, Chase Bank, Digital Equipment, The U.S. General Services Administration and Department of Agriculture, Mobil, Pepsico, Procter & Gamble, Shell and Whirlpool among many others. He is the co-author of another best-selling book in this series, "WORKING TOGETHER."

Ms. Weissman brings to her consulting and speaking a rich 15 year industry experience in male and female dominated industries such as health care, finance, food and beverage and theater. She has a broad management experience which includes general management, marketing, training, budget analysis, purchasing, contract and negotiations in both labor and service.

INTRODUCTION

We all desire to do good work. We also expect to be recognized and rewarded for it. Imagine how productive we could be if, as women and men, we were able to put insight, skills, and energy into doing our personal best, both in our jobs and our ability to work together.

Unfortunately, for many of us, this is an unfulfilled vision. Never in history have men and women worked side-by-side in such an uneasy truce as they do today. Women complain of unfairness, harassment, abuse, and careers which bump against a ''glass ceiling''—where they can see the top, but can't get there. Men argue that women don't play by the rules, can't be trusted, and are ''out to get them.'' Yet the collaboration of women and men in the workplace is more than a matter of justice or a luxury in today's world. From now on finding, hiring, managing, training and retaining a mixed workforce is the only available road to success for major organizations.

Gender conflict in the workplace reflects what goes on in our homes and hearts as we learn new roles as mates, companions, and friends. When we fail to meet each other's expectations, we blame and punish instead of looking for ways to understand each other and make agreements that last. We become upset and resentful, rather than curious, understanding, and creative when working together.

This book invites you to view working together and resolving conflict as challenges that you can meet by developing awareness and skill, rather than as political or psychological problems. It provides you with a set of productive communication tools for everyday use.

To work well with each other, there are ten tasks to accomplish. Each section of this book will help you master one of them. We challenge you to a new vision of partnership—you can turn the pain and confusion which women and men experience on the job into personal power, support for each other, and into professional excellence together.

So, sit down, grab a pencil and get to work. It's time to make a change.

George F. Simons

G. Deborah Weissman

GETTING THE MOST FROM THIS BOOK

What do we want from each other as women and men working together? What would we like to change about how we relate to each other now? What skills do we need to make a difference? These are questions you should ask as you start this book.

Below is a list of possible learning goals. Read them and check those which could be personal goals. If you do this thoughtfully, what you check will help you focus on what you need and enable you to get more from each section of the book.

- ☐ I want to experience less tension, pain, or blame and be more at ease working with people of the other sex.

- ☐ I want to acquire skills I can use everyday on the job to resolve my conflicts with members of the other sex.

- ☐ I want to understand how women and men are different.

- ☐ I want to stop beating around the bush and be clear with the other sex about what I expect from them.

- ☐ I want to treat members of the other sex fairly and be treated fairly by them.

- ☐ I want to break through ''the glass ceiling'' which limits my career.

- ☐ I want to know why people are so worked up about women's and men's issues.

- ☐ I want to encourage both women and men in my organization to make the best use of their abilities and become star performers.

- ☐ I am committed to fairness and equality and want to know how to go about it in a better way.

- ☐ I want my relationships with members of the other sex to be in line with my professional and personal values and commitments.

- ☐ _____

CONTENTS

Contents (Continued)

THE TEN TASKS COVERED IN THIS BOOK

TASK 1. **Know the issues** facing both women and men in the workplace and why those issues are critical in the organization of the future.

TASK 2. **Learn how people and organizations develop** their awareness of gender issues and the skills to deal with them.

TASK 3. **Accept gender differences** in ways that enable you to overcome stereotypes and deal realistically with each other.

TASK 4. **Speak with respect,** recognizing differences in how women and men talk and express their emotions. Avoid words and behaviors that might offend, exclude, or put others down.

TASK 5. **Learn from each other** so that you can both use the skills which have been traditionally looked at as belonging to only one sex or the other.

TASK 6. **Create understanding** by mastering two skills which will help you listen better to each other and clear up misunderstandings.

TASK 7. **Create agreements** and know what to do when commitments break down.

TASK 8. **Collaborate** by knowing how male and female differences affect us as managers and subordinates.

TASK 9. **Pay attention to each other** by giving each other recognition and managing the male-female tensions which come from working side by side.

TASK 10. **Find and use resources** that can help you personally continue to learn and assist your organization to function more effectively.

KNOW THE ISSUES

The workplace is changing. More of us than ever before in history are holding jobs side-by-side with the other sex. Career opportunities are different today, and promotions are fewer. Despite efforts made in recent years, we still experience conflict and unfair standards. In this section we will look at how these changes affect us personally as men and women working together.

WOMEN'S ISSUES, MEN'S ISSUES

What makes it tough for women and men to work together productively?

The checklists below contain some common ''issues.'' Read the list that pertains to you as a man or woman. Check ✔ the items that you feel most affect you. Then read the other list and check the concerns which you believe are important to people of the other sex in your organization. If possible compare your list with someone of the other sex who is doing this exercise.

You will notice that some items sound the same in both lists, e.g., ''Low self esteem.'' Both men and women can feel badly about themselves at work. On the other hand ''how'' a man feels badly, what he says to himself and how he acts may differ greatly from how a woman feels, thinks, and acts. Many men attempt to cover their loss of pride by looking tough or macho, whereas many women start doubting their ability to succeed.

Women's Issues

☐ Feel misunderstood and put down by men.

☐ Less pay for the same work.

☐ Slower or non-existent promotions compared to men.

☐ Receive less feedback and information on the job than men do.

☐ Unwanted sexual attention (words, advances, touches).

☐ Being left out of decision making.

☐ Low self-esteem.

☐ Inability to assert oneself and be heard.

☐ Fewer training opportunities.

☐ _____

Men's Issues

☐ Feeling misunderstood and put down by women.

☐ More susceptible to stress related diseases.

☐ Deprived of home and family time.

☐ "Workaholism"—being addicted to work.

☐ Unwanted sexual attention (dress, flirtatious behavior).

☐ Low self esteem.

☐ Tired of competing all the time.

☐ Forced into narrow and specialized niches.

☐ Not allowed to make mistakes or admit you don't know.

☐ _____

Why Now?

During the past quarter of a century there has been a major transformation of men's and women's roles in the workplace. In some organizations it is believed that one's sex no longer plays a significant part in what happens to an individual at work. On the other hand, in analyzing more than ten years of first hand experience with American organizations, one group of experts found:

> *...an inner world in individuals and organizations that can best be described with the word: "chaos."*
>
> *Men and women who work together on a day-to-day basis—when explored in depth about their feelings, opinions, ideas and concerns—are befuddled, confused, ignorant and grossly unskilled in understanding how best to work with each other.*
>
> *After centuries of living together in families and other institutions, men and women in the modern working world simply do not know each other any more—how to talk to each other, what each other's basic life-expectations are, how to support and trust each other.*
>
> *Partners in Chaos*

What Is Your Experience?

As you see it, what things have become better for women and men working together? Write your answer in the space below.

_____

_____

_____

_____

_____

What opportunities and problems do you think still lie beneath the surface?

_____

_____

_____

_____

_____

Why Do Gender Issues Continue To Exist?

Although laws about equal opportunity, sexual harrassment, and affirmative action have been passed in different states and countries, they address only some of the most flagrant abuses of people's right to fairness. People are reluctant or afraid to come forth and complain. Violations are often difficult to prove and standards are costly to enforce.

Some organizations try to improve the quality of worklife for both sexes. They create their own guidelines and encourage employees to discuss and propose solutions to women's and, more recently, men's issues. This is slow going and sometimes seems to raise more problems than it solves.

REASONS PEOPLE GIVE

Following is a list of reasons people give for a lack of progress. Put the letter **F** in front of those you believe are facts and an **A** in front of those you think are attitudes people could change if they knew how.

_____ Men can't see women's problems because they are not affected by them.

_____ The problem's too big. Things would get out of hand if we tried to deal with man-woman issues.

_____ The "war between the sexes" has gone on since time began. It won't stop now.

_____ There are too few models of what a successful man-woman workforce should look like.

_____ Women will never be satisfied.

_____ We have good will, but we simply don't know how to do it.

_____ It would cause even more division.

_____ It's not the job of an organization like this to try to reform society.

_____ Women and men are different from each other and there's nothing we can do about it.

_____ Business is business and people just have to fit in or get out.

_____ We're already doing all we can.

_____ These problems affect the older generation, not us.

OBSTACLES AND ISSUES

What obstacles to better female-male collaboration do you feel exist or do you hear people talk about in your organization?

_____

_____

_____

_____

_____

The truth is that gender issues continue to exist at some level in virtually every organization because of changes in society and/or technology advances. We have only begun to feel the effects of new roles, new tools, and new organizational structures which will revolutionize the workplace of the future.

Sex roles are visibly shifting and will continue to shift as women approach 50% of the workforce. Women will very often work in organizations whose policies and unwritten rules were designed for men and by men. This creates problems because many women have special needs connected with commitments to home and family. Also, as thousands of immigrants and non-whites of both sexes enter the workforce, white males (whose numbers and values dominated the workforce for so long) are becoming a minority. A male manufacturing supervisor described it like this:

> _I don't know when it happened, but it seems like I woke up one day and realized that everything had changed. My boss was a woman and I was no longer working with the kind of people I grew up with. I've worked here twenty-two years but it seems like a strange place to me now._

In a similar way, a woman hotel manager groused:

> _We women have struggled so long and so hard for the places we now hold. What will become of us as more and more organizations come under the ownership of foreigners whose culture seems to me to be far more oppressive to women than ours?_

WHAT CHANGES HAVE YOU NOTICED?

How have the people who work in your organization or manage it changed in the past five years? What effect has this had on how you feel about yourself as a woman or a man?

_____

_____

_____

Economics and new technology often force companies to downsize and reduce levels of management. Many of us now work in smaller, more entrepreneurial organizations where networking, teamwork, and communicating effectively with people who are different are as essential as traditional line management skills, like planning, organizing and controlling.*

How have the skills needed to work in your organization changed in the last five years? Or, if you have changed jobs, what new changes do you see in the way your organization or others you know of now operates?

_____

_____

Though climbing a career ladder is still a normal expectation for most men and a fiercely sought goal for many women, it will be harder to do because middle management jobs are rapidly disappearing. Men and women, who do not learn to collaborate and find satisfaction as working partners, are primed for disappointment and conflict. As one top executive put it:

> _Promotions are going to be more rare for both sexes. The ''glass ceiling'' which women speak of—being able to see the top but not get there—will be even harder to penetrate. Lack of advancement will strike another blow at men's egos. More initiative will be required. People who lack the skills of working effectively with the other sex will be misfits. The winners will be those who find their perks in creativity and teamwork._

Has your organization or one you know of recently undergone ''downsizing''? How has that affected the way men and women work together?

_____

_____

---

* For an excellent book on this topic, order _Working Together_ using the information in the back of this book.

DOUBLE STANDARDS

When one sex is dominant in the workforce, individuals who are in the minority often encounter a double standard. Here are some examples:

Male Report:

When I first arrived as the only male on the office staff of a property management firm, the women made a point of telling me, "You have to get your own coffee and wash your own dishes, just like we do." Yet every time a truck arrived with a heavy haul, they told the driver to call me to help carry in the load, because I was the only "boy." One day a female driver showed up, looked at the receptionist and said, "Come on, honey, this doesn't take brawn it just takes effort!"

Female Report:

It drives me nuts when the men apologize for swearing in front of a woman. They don't do that if only men are present. Also, men test women in ways they don't test men. A man will start with a "damn," then escalate to a slightly off-color joke, and get progressively fouler, always checking for my reaction. If a woman dares talk like that, she is immediately called a "witch," whereas he's still just "one of the boys."

A double standard exists when one group of people is told that they are to be treated in all respects like those in the dominant group, but in actuality are treated differently and usually unfairly. There are, in fact, two standards, one for men and one for women, though people don't admit it. Double standards create double binds—you find yourself "damned-if-you-do," and "damned-if-you-don't."

In the space on the top of the facing page, list those double standards which you experience or have seen others experience at work. Then in the space provided, describe one "double standard" in detail, with the double binds it creates. Show what the unwritten rules are and how they make it difficult for people to work together productively. Later, you will find a formula for dealing with double standards that you encounter at work or in your private life.

Double Standards Which I Encounter in My Organization:

1. _____
   _____
   _____

2. _____
   _____
   _____

3. _____
   _____
   _____

Here Are The Problems Caused By One of Them:

_____
_____
_____
_____
_____
_____
_____

OVERTURNING A DOUBLE STANDARD

To overcome a double standard you must first become aware of it, point it out, and then negotiate with the people who are able to make a change. These five questions will help you:

1. **What's going on?** Identify the double standard. Write down what takes place.

I am told that I am to be equally responsible for the decisions we make. Yet I do not get invited to certain meetings where decisions are being made. They are telling me one thing but treating me the opposite.

2. **When does it happen?** Recognize the situations in which a standard contradictory to the one stated is applied.

Often decisions are made in informal after-hours sessions to which I am not invited or which are held at the club where I am not a member.

3. **Who is the target group?** Find out who besides yourself is experiencing what you are. If there are others, get their collaboration to put a stop to it.

I am (We men/women are) being told one thing and treated in another way. Is that true for you as well? Do we agree that this is the situation? Are we determined to make a change? What is our strategy?

4. **What changes will I (we) insist on?** Discuss the double standard with the individual or group that practices it. Create an agreement to point out when it occurs and negotiate a process for change, one which will meet the needs of both parties.

I want you to tell me when you intend to discuss decisions outside of regular working hours. I either expect to be there or give you my input. I want you to either invite me or agree not to come to final decisions without discussing them with me. In return I promise to support the outcomes of our decision-making process whole heartedly. Do you agree to that?

5. What progress is being made? Once the person or group has agreed to make changes, support them by giving them a regular "report card" which applauds their efforts and helps them see where improvement can still be made.

You've been doing a great job at keeping me informed about after hours meetings, but I'm concerned about the changes you made when you and Sam got together last weekend.

Change a Double Standard That Affects You

Answer the following questions and make a promise to yourself to deal with a double standard that affects you or others where you work.

What's going on? _____

_____

_____

When is it happening? _____

_____

_____

Who is the target group? _____

_____

_____

What changes will I (we) insist on? _____

_____

_____

What progress is being made?

Date: _____ _____

_____ _____

_____ _____

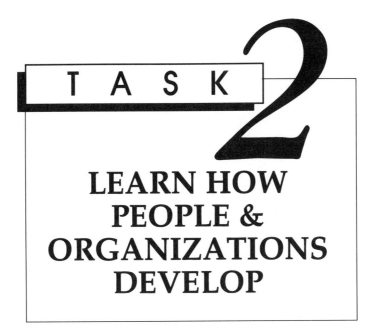

T A S K **2**

LEARN HOW PEOPLE & ORGANIZATIONS DEVELOP

To form productive partnerships people and their organizations go through stages of development. For example, they become aware of problems caused by traditional gender roles and stereotypes. They react to these problems and begin to take responsibility for making changes. In this section you will learn what these stages are and find out what to do when you encounter them.

STAGES ON THE WAY TO PARTNERSHIP

Men and women who know how to work together and organizations that help them learn about working together are most likely to succeed both today and in the future. Those that do not will be tomorrow's losers.

Conflict between women and men and frustration with double standards can become opportunities if they alert us to our problems and lead us to action. This is not easy. It requires us to be honest about what we are experiencing, clear about what we want, and fearless in confronting ourselves, each other, and our values. We go through certain stages in doing this. These stages can be predicted, recognized, and handled if we know something about them beforehand.

Organizational development specialists have charted the steps through which men and women pass when traditional gender roles are in conflict.[1] The stages for individuals as well as those of organizations are listed side by side on the facing page. This does not mean that the stages take place simultaneously, are the same for all individuals and organizations, or that individuals and organizations go through every stage in this order, but they frequently do.

Because traditional gender roles subordinate women to men, women are usually the ones who first become aware that something is unfair or not working for them. Then, it usually takes women's anger at a double standard or complaints of harrassment, discrimination, or unfairness for an organization to become aware and take action.

Men tend to react to changes in women's attitudes toward them personally or blame the changes on "organizational pressures." Later, astute men discover that traditional roles and stereotypes cost them something, too.

---

[1]This model is based on the work of Judith Palmer, Carol Pierce, David Wagner, John McPherson and Bill Gregory. More about these stages can be found by reading the books listed in the Resources in Task 10.

WOMEN'S STAGES	ORGANIZATIONAL REACTIONS TO GENDER ISSUES	MEN'S STAGES
UNAWARE Innocent of the issues & their impact on self & others.		UNAWARE Innocent of the issues & their impact on self & others.
	UNAWARE Does not recognize that gender issues play any role in the workplace.	
DENIAL There are no women's issues, or, they do not pertain to me.		RANDOM DATA COLLECTION What's going on here?
	DENIAL If gender issues exist, they do not pertain to our relationships or this organization, or gender issues are personal, they are not the work of this organization.	DENIAL Women's issues may exist but they don't apply to me.
AWAKENING Something is happening. What's it all about?		
		CRITICAL INCIDENT Emotional event leads to systematic data collection.
IDENTIFICATION Women's issues are real and they are my issues.	CRITICAL INCIDENT Lawsuit, boycott, adverse publicity, loss of women employees, etc.	IDENTIFICATION Women's issues are real and they are my issues, too.
ANGER • RAGE Men deprive us of power, visibility, competence, independence.	REACTION This can't be happening to us! Do something! (usually to avoid, attack, or "fix" the situation).	ANGER • GUILT What has society, with my complicity done to me!? How can I fix it?
FEAR • WITHDRAWAL I'm afraid. I feel helpless. It's hopeless. Men are no good.	PATTERN RECOGNITION The issues are ours & they are part of our system.	GRIEF • ACCEPTANCE I can share & bear the loss with other men.
CONFRONTING ISSUES I will take steps on my own and seek support of other women.	BUREAUCRACY The task is too big, too risky. Put someone in charge. Let's move slowly, cautiously.	ACTION With other men I can develop what's missing for me.
POWER is within me & can be shared. I can make things happen.	VISION We can adopt new values, make this a different organization. Managing diversity's a condition for future success.	POWER I am more than my roles. I can be powerful, playful and wise.
	ACTION We will change the system & train people.	

PARTNERSHIP & PRODUCTIVITY

TIPS FOR MEN

Dealing with Changing Women

Following are the stages from the model on page 15 that women pass through and some tips about how to behave toward those in each stage. Check ✓ those stages which contain tips you particularly need to practice.

☐ **UNAWARE** Not conscious of the issues. Few women today seem to be truly unaware of women's issues once they become teenagers. **Tip:** *Talk about gender issues as facts of life, honestly and openly.*

☐ **DENIAL** "I know that the issues exist, but certainly not in our group." "Never in all my years with the company have I been discriminated against because I am a woman." Many women tend to be ambivalent: they want to confront, but have been culturally conditioned to nurture. Denial feels safe. **Tip:** *Be matter of fact about gender issues. Do not try to argue her into "seeing the light."*

☐ **AWAKENING** Something happens that gets her thinking. She starts to look around herself and talk with other women. **Tip:** *Listen to her questions. Answer honestly. Do not blame her for being interested in women's issues or for being less aware than other women.*

☐ **IDENTIFICATION** She realizes that "this is about *me*," and sees herself as part of a distinct cultural group— women. She begins to see the rest of the world from this new perspective. She studies, talks, and shares. Her social philosophy and criticism of men is idealistic and general, though she is unlikely to attack individual men. **Tip:** *Listen patiently and deal with her as with anyone enthusiastic over something new. Avoid the temptation to debate and make her wrong. Encourage her to learn more, see more sides to issues. Maintain your own self-esteem—her global assertions about men can leave you feeling helpless and enraged. Don't defend men as a group. Accept what might be true in her criticism.*

☐ **ANGER • RAGE** She sees even more deeply how unfair her position as a woman is and how overwhelming the forces are that maintain it. Her anger is directed at authority which upholds the system. She feels men are the enemy and is also angry with women who appear to collaborate. **Tip:** *This is a necessary and critical stage wherein a woman begins to claim her power. It is a particularly difficult time for women because anger has often been a forbidden emotion. It is equally difficult for men because they are no longer in control of the situation. Listen actively without attacking, defending, and especially avoid trying to "fix" the situation. Be in control of yourself, not of her.*

TIPS FOR MEN (Continued)

☐ **FEAR • WITHDRAWAL** The more she ''sees'' the more powerless she feels to do anything. If the cost of change seems too high, she withdraws, and returns to an outward form of denial to protect herself from danger, while unconsciously rejecting all men as sexist and untrustworthy. **Tip:** *Do what you can to make her feel safe both in the relationship and the environment and to connect her with women who can support her. Without this support many women can vacillate between anger and withdrawal for many years.*

☐ **CONFRONTING ISSUES** She becomes grounded in the world around her, understands its dynamics, and realizes that it is up to her to make a difference in her life. She accepts the challenge of confrontation in a personal, empowering way. She is ready to work for change with other women and even men. **Tip:** *Prepare yourself to accept both confrontation and collaboration. Be aware of using excuses and stereotypes as ways to avoid sharing power.*

☐ **POWER** Having developed a clear sense of identity as a woman and as a member of the working world, she gradually loses ''self-consciousness'' as a woman and strengthens awareness of herself as an individual. She is now more able than ever before to form meaningful, productive, and co-equal work relationships with men. **Tip:** *This woman will have a clear sense of boundaries and will let you know if you have transgressed them. Do not confuse this with anger or defensiveness. Support these women wherever you find them. They will actively intervene in the workplace to champion and model co-equality.*

Respect women in whatever stage they may be even though they don't seem to respect you.

It is never helpful to say, ''This is just a stage you're going through.'' Such ''put downs'' say that you value neither her nor her experience. They send the message that you are unwilling to change and grow and cannot accept change and growth on the part of others.

Women will swing back and forth between stages of development. Don't demand that they always be consistent.

These are all necessary steps on the path to personal power.

TIPS FOR WOMEN

Dealing with Changing Men Here are the stages from the model on page 15 that men pass through and some tips for dealing with them. Check ✓ those stages which contain tips you need to practice.

☐ **UNAWARE** As a member of the dominant culture the gender issues which impact him and the people around him are invisible. "The world is as it should be," and he is happy in his innocence. **Tip:** *See this as a normal starting point and do not dispair, men can change.*

☐ **RANDOM DATA COLLECTION** He starts to pick up clues of what is going on around him. A few angry words, a complaint, something his wife said... He is cautiously curious. Spurts of machismo keep him safe. **Tip:** *Feed him information a little at a time, facts, hard data, rather than opinions.*

☐ **DENIAL** "Maybe the issues are real, but it certainly doesn't apply to me (us)! If he is well connected to other men like himself, he will joke about it with them and brush it off. If he is alienated from other men, he may point to them (not himself) as the problem. **Tip:** *Connect him to other men who will not support his denial. If he is close only to women, do not let him get away with telling you he is different.*

☐ **CRITICAL INCIDENT** He has a "significant emotional event," often anger or abandonment from women close to him. Now he wants to get to the bottom of it so he can avoid other such incidents. At first he easily slips back into denial, but the evidence begins to stack up. **Tip:** *Stand by him without betraying the woman who triggered the incident. If you are the woman, don't make light of what you did or said.*

☐ **IDENTIFICATION** The evidence is overwhelming. Women's issues are real and he is not only affected by them but also involved in and responsible for devaluing women. He is vaguely aware that this costs him something as well. **Tip:** *Invite him to talk about it but avoid, "I told you so!"*

☐ **ANGER • GUILT** He is angry at himself, society, other men, women who played along, his parents, even God. Angry that he can no longer avoid the issue and is cut off from men who do. "What have I done?" "How can I (or other men) be any good?" "What can I do?" "How can I pay attention to this and continue living a normal life?" **Tip:** *Do not be afraid of his anger, listen actively without probing for what you would like to hear but don't. Encourage him to talk to other men who have gone through this stage.*

TIPS FOR WOMEN (Continued)

☐ **GRIEF • ACCEPTANCE** He begins to accept things as they are, along with his imperfections. Realizing he alone is not accountable for the history and behavior of all men toward women, he commits to do what he can. Sharing his experience with other men, he discovers others who feel the same and becomes aware of how traditional roles have victimized men as well as women. He sees his manliness as both dignified and wounded. **Tip:** *Applaud his new involvement with other men. Avoid the temptation to distrust this as a return to male chauvinism.*

☐ **ACTION** He becomes aware that men's and women's issues are separate but related. He recognizes that women's agenda for men may not be his own, but he can learn from women's experiences. He now has energy to redefine himself and to work with other men to create standards for a new kind of maleness. **Tip:** *Old means of controlling him no longer work, but his is much more available for negotiating agreements for change.*

☐ **POWER** He starts to experience real power (not machismo) as his values and actions become aligned. He no longer "walks on eggs" around women or women's issues. Able to identify potential as well as actual issues, he can take the initiative to negotiate with someone who is "different" without needing to be in control. **Tip:** *This man is for you but the power he exercises can be disturbing and you may sometimes confuse it with machismo. He will actively intervene in the workplace to champion and model co-equality.*

Respect men at whatever stage they may be even though they don't seem to respect you.

Be both insistent and patient. Because organizations tend to embody male values and fill many of men's needs, it is difficult for men to see the need for change. When it comes to articulating their own concerns men are frequently isolated. The men's movement is much younger than the women's movement and male support for men can be much harder to find.

Men will swing back and forth between stages of development. Don't expect them to always be consistent.

When men get stuck, it tends to be in the earlier stages. Unaware, Random Data Collection and Denial. Anger as an emotional outlet should not be confused with the Anger Stage itself.

TIPS FOR ORGANIZATIONS

Dealing with Organizations

As seen in the model on page 15, organizations go through a series of steps in dealing with gender issues. Because of the male history of so many organizations, the steps tend to parallel male stages more than female stages. As you read through the stages below, check ✓ those which contain tips you need to act on.

☐ UNAWARE

Organizations are legally required to know and comply with certain standards of equal opportunity and affirmative action. However many organizations are unaware of how day-to-day gender issues actually affect their people. **Tip:** *Familiarize yourself with the law and your company's policies. Then observe how people are talked to and talked about as women and men. Observe how the sexes treat each other. Where do you see discomfort and hostility?*

☐ DENIAL

Most organizations tend to deny that gender issues are a serious concern. They concentrate instead on doing whatever they were organized to do. Usually, it's making a profit for company and stockholders. They claim that gender issues are not the responsibility of the organization or make the assumption that someone in the organization is taking care of this. **Tip:** *Facts, facts, facts. Talk about what is taking place in terms of what people are actually doing, saying, and experiencing as a result of organizational policies, structures, and attitudes.*

☐ CRITICAL INCIDENT

When a critical incident occurs that threatens the organization's productivity, profitability, or public image, the organization is rudely awakened from its denial. Examples would be: the threat of boycott, a sexual harassment suit, or equal opportunity violation. **Tip:** *Try to get "the bigger picture" which shows that this is not an isolated incident. Share this picture with others.*

☐ REACTION

The furor around the critical incident is often greeted by disbelief—"This can't be happening to us." Then the organization reacts with more denial to cover its tracks, while it makes efforts to control the damage and "fix" the situation. It also takes precautions that similar incidents do not recur. New rules and regulations aimed at keeping people in line fall short of changing attitudes and teaching new skills. So, when new stresses arise, people fall into old habits and more critical incidents occur. **Tip:** *Resist a one-sided blaming approach, i.e., this is a "women's" or a "men's" problem. Get both sexes to collaborate in finding solutions. (It's also a good time to get groups of people to study this book!)*

TIPS FOR CHANGING ORGANIZATIONS (Continued)

☐ **PATTERN RECOGNITION** Finally the organization recognizes that a pattern exists. That critical incidents are not just accidents but will continue to happen because of the values and structure of the organization itself. **Tip:** *Keep a journal of what happens, how often and to whom. Discuss what you see with others and look for connections between their experiences and your perceptions.*

☐ **BUREAUCRACY** Once a pattern is clear, the organization has one more temptation to overcome. Though a great deal of anger and guilt may be engendered as people see what has been taking place, they may fear the consequences of taking action. The task is too big, or too risky for individuals. Committees are appointed to study the situation. Publications appear. **Tip:** *Take personal responsibility for making changes in your environment. Encourage people to discuss issues openly.*

☐ **VISION** A leader must articulate a vision of a different kind of workplace if an organization is to succeed in gender related issues. This is a top management responsibility but the vision requires leadership at every level in the organization. **Tip:** *If you are not now a leader, you become one by having a vision and sharing it with others.*

☐ **ACTION** Now the organization is ready to take action that will change the system and train and reward employees for becoming competent in dealing with the other sex. Managing gender issues becomes everybody's responsibililty. **Tip:** *If your organization has reached this stage, take advantage of new opportunities to learn and acquire skills. Continue to take personal responsibility for progress in this area.*

Why are male-female issues so difficult to deal with? First of all, they cut deeply. They force us to ask ourselves who we are and how we should act.

Secondly, although individuals and culture are slowly changing their values; people and organizations may be in different stages. You can't draw a straight line across the diagram on page 15 and assume everyone fits the picture. Some people believe change is ''moving at a snail's pace,'' while others shout, ''Slow down!'' Still others sigh for ''the good old days, when men were men and women were women.''

Changing an organization is never over. New people, new tasks, and new challenges arrive daily. The culture people experience outside the organization may make them fall into old habits or resist change.

Denial and Bureaucracy are the stages in which organizations are likely to be stuck.

WHY ARE THE STAGES IMPORTANT?

- **They help you recognize, understand, and accept reactions and emotions that you experience as you face gender conflict, absorb new information, and try to learn new skills.** The fact that you are working through this book indicates you are at least curious. As you continue you will find the stages make more sense, and you will see new ways to understand others. You may also advance from denial to action on issues that you have not dealt with before. *Go back to the chart on page 15 and circle the stage you feel you are in. Then ask others if they would agree.*

- **They help you recognize, understand, and accept the feelings and behavior of others.** You probably work with people who are at different stages. Some deliberately choose to stay at certain levels. Others lack the insights, resources, or support to move on. Many get stuck at one stage for long periods. *Look at the chart again. Does it suggest why some of your relationships with people you work with are the way they are?*

- **They serve as a guide to what we must be do personally and organizationally to provide what's missing to integrate women and men in the workplace.** *Where on the chart on page 15 do you feel your organization stands? Put a star there. Discuss this chart with colleagues and get their reactions. What stages do their reactions suggest?*

The most important thing I have learned in this section is:

_____

_____

Here is the first step I will personally take to help me get to the next stage.

_____

_____

Here is one step I will take to help change my organization.

_____

_____

T A S K 3

ACCEPT GENDER DIFFERENCES

As men and women (and as individuals), our bodies and minds have been shaped differently by biology and culture. In this section we will examine traditional cultural messages or stereotypes about being male and female to learn how they limit us and to get a fresh look at how we can change them.

A FRESH LOOK AT OLD PROBLEMS

In many organizations differences and conflicts between women and men are either swept under the rug or one side blames the other. This is particularly true when people are in the stages of denial or anger. You hear attitudes like those in the list below. Put your initial by any of the attitudes which you have held. Check ✔ those which are common in your organization. Then, using the diagram on page 15, indicate what stage you feel each statement represents.

Initials	✔	Stage	Statement
			There's really no problem. Men and women in our organization get along fine.
			It's all men's fault. They're too dominant.
			Why make a fuss about differences? We're all basically the same—just human beings—aren't we?
			Let it work itself out. It just takes time. You can't expect too much progress in too short a time.
			It's too dangerous to deal with this issue. Nobody can win, and there's too much to lose.
			It's women's fault. They shouldn't be competing with men.
			We never had a problem until we started getting those company statements and booklets about equal opportunity and harassment.
			Women are too sensitive—they don't understand that things can be said in fun. They overreact.
			The war between the sexes is eternal. Working together is no different from living together when it comes to getting along.

Avoiding and blaming are a last-ditch stand. We resort to them when we don't have the information attitudes or skills to do anything else. Critical incidents will continue to happen, at great cost to organizations and employees, unless we get a new perspective. In this section we will take a fresh look at the differences and strengths of women and men from the point of view of culture and language.

WE'RE ALWAYS TALKING ABOUT SEX

Sex is the first and most fundamental distinction made about human beings. We are conceived and born male or female. This biological difference sets us apart more than any single characteristic. It makes our bodies look and behave differently. Being born black or white, Canadian or Japanese, Muslim or Christian, rich or poor normally has less impact on our lives than the first words spoken when we are born, ''It's a girl!'' or, ''It's a boy!''

FACT	*Nature* **makes us biologically different as men and women. Our** *sex* **makes us** *male* **or** *female* **in every cell and every function of our body.**

Because of our sex, we are brought up in distinctly different cultures. People talk and gesture to us, touch us, and look at us differently. They dress us differently and assign us different values, ideals and roles. We imitate them and start talking to ourselves as they talked to us. As a result, men and women grow up to think, feel and act differently. We find different things right or wrong, beautiful or ugly, true or false.

FACT	*Culture* **builds on nature's distinction between female and male. It puts each of us into a** *social class* **and teaches us how to be** *feminine* **or** *masculine.*

For years people have argued the question, *Where does nature end and culture begin?* They were really trying to answer many other far more important questions like those listed below. What answers would you give these questions?

How different are women and men really?

_____

_____

_____

Should we be treated differently or not?

_____

_____

_____

WE'RE ALWAYS TALKING ABOUT SEX (Continued)

How fair is it to treat us differently?

_____

_____

How much of our male or female thinking and behavior can we control?

_____

_____

How much and how quickly can we change if we want to?

_____

_____

How deep do masculine and feminine traits run?

_____

_____

Is one sex better or superior to the other? If so, how?

_____

_____

What can we do that the other sex can't?

_____

_____

 FACT **Both nature and culture are intimately connected to each other. Both layers operate at once. We may not agree on the answers to these questions, but we all have opinions on them and these opinions shape how we think, act, and feel toward each other.**

FACT **Our culture has long told us that ''different'' always means ''inferior'' or ''unequal,'' especially if we are dealing with people different from ourselves or those not part of the dominant culture in which we live. When we change this thinking we will be able to enjoy the rich diversity which the sexes bring to each other and to their work.**

HOW WE TALK TO OURSELVES ABOUT BEING MEN & WOMEN

How did we get the way we are? Most of us were told in no uncertain terms about what a woman or a man was, and how to behave if we were to be ''good'' boys and girls who would grow up to be ''real'' men or women. These messages came and continue to come from all directions. They shape what we call ''stereotypes,'' the common images we unconsciously use to define what is male or female or to judge what is okay and not okay for us as men or women.

If you listen, you can hear these messages echo in your mind. Listen to them as you finish each of the statements below. This will give you a sense of how deeply messages are imprinted on your mind. Don't try to think up answers. Just read the phrase, listen to what your mind says, and write it down. Do this five times in rapid succession for each phrase:

Women are . . .   Men are . . .

_____   _____

_____   _____

_____   _____

_____   _____

_____   _____

Good boys . . .   Good girls . . .

_____   _____

_____   _____

_____   _____

_____   _____

HOW WE TALK ABOUT OURSELVES (Continued)

A real man is . . .

_____

_____

_____

_____

A real woman is . . .

_____

_____

_____

_____

When I am around women, I should . . .

_____

_____

_____

_____

When I am around men, I should . . .

_____

_____

_____

_____

What was your reaction to doing this exercise? Check those that fit for you.

☐ It was very easy to do—I could have gone on for a page or two.

☐ It surprised me to hear my mind still say some of those things.

☐ I struggled a bit—old messages are in conflict with messages I am getting now.

☐ I'm sure most people still think this way.

(Add other thoughts)

_____

_____

FACT Whether we like it or not, early messages about what it means to be a woman or a man are permanently stored and always at work in our minds. When we are threatened or afraid these early messages become very strong because we feel safe with them.

WARNING

BEFORE YOU GO FURTHER

No one human is a ''typical'' man or woman. Though biology and culture create female and male traits that can be measured for groups, each individual combines these traits in his or her own unique way. If we assume we know what others are like, we stereotype them. Treating them on the basis of stereotypes is unfair. Our challenge is to get to know, value, and learn to work with each other as individuals.

PROCEED WITH CAUTION

HOW STEREOTYPES WORK

No two of us have received exactly the same training in how to be women or men. Still, despite recent changes in how women and men are asked to behave at work and at home, it is clear that most of us have grown up with deeply rooted traditional messages about who we are as men and women and how we are to play masculine and feminine roles. Many of these traditional messages work against us.

This traditional programming is reinforced by how women and men are pictured in movies, ads, and television shows, and by the everyday words and actions of people around us. If you want to know how many days of gender progamming you have received, multiply your age in years by 365!

This programming operates beneath the surface of our conscious minds—we don't even notice it, yet we live by it. What messages make up female and male identity in our culture and how do they affect our working together? Let's look at the most basic ones.

I must RELATE to others to survive.

I must COMPETE with others to survive.

BASIC SURVIVAL MESSAGE

HOW STEREOTYPES WORK
(Continued)

Many studies have documented how our culture causes women and men to differ in their basic orientation to life, but the following observation from an ex-teacher says it most eloquently:

> *Building relationships is, for women, a goal in itself. Men see it as a way to get other things done. You can see the difference if you watch how little girls and little boys play. When the girls get into a disagreement, they have to resolve it then and there. Relationships have to become harmonious before they can go back to playing together. But boys—they don't have any problem playing with boys they don't like. Usually boy's games have rules for resolving differences and conflicts fairly and impersonally.*

The basic survival messages automatically tell us what is good or bad for us. We use them unconsciously to size up people and situations. We measure our success and shape our future plans by them. They also sabotage us when we try to set goals for ourselves that do not square with traditional gender messages inside us.

Men and women are told what is important for them in life and are taught to feel good to the degree they succeed in getting these priorities met. The following diagrams show the most common priorities our society assigns to each sex:

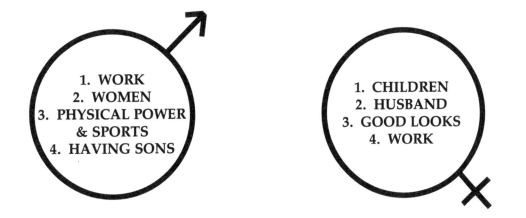

From these fundamental messages and priorities emerges the whole spectrum of traditional masculine and feminine thinking and behavior. It tells us who we are and includes the expectations we have about how both our sex and the other sex should behave.

COMMON GENDER STEREOTYPES

Below are lists of common female and male stereotypes which flow from the basic survival messages of women and men. Compare this list with the inner messages you wrote down on pages 27 and 28.

Women are:	Men are:	When we act as if these stereotypes were the whole truth, what are the consequences for women and men at work?
Dependent	Independent	_____
Weak	Powerful	
Incompetent	Competent	_____
Less important	More important	
Emotional	Logical	_____
Implementors	Decision Makers	
Housekeepers	Breadwinners	_____
Supporters	Leaders	
Fragile	Protectors	_____
Fickle	Consistent	
Fearful	Brave	_____
Nice	Aggressive	
Cautious	Adventurous	_____
Flexible	Focused	
Warm	Self-reliant	_____
Passive	Active	
Followers	Leaders	_____
Spectators	Doers	
Modest	Ambitious	_____
Subjective	Objective	
Softspoken	Outspoken	_____
Secretaries	Bosses	
Nurturing	Assertive	_____
Gentle	Strong	
Excitable	Stoical	_____
Patient	Impetuous	
Cheerful	Forceful	_____
Sensitive	Brave	
Caretakers	Achievers	_____
Cooperative	Competitive	
		_____
		_____

COMMON STEREOTYPES (Continued)

Stereotypes are self-fulfilling prophecies. Told that ''real men'' are strong, competitive, task oriented, logical, aggressive, outspoken, etc., we males may work very hard at acting just that way. Likewise, told that ''real women'' are to prize relationships, be sensitive to others, giving, empathetic, cooperative, feeling, etc., we females do our best to become so.

Stereotypes are at work in all of us. Despite the trouble they cause, they are important because they provide information we need to grow up and acquire skills and strengths. Simply having stereotypes is not the problem—we all do to some extent. They become a problem when we use them to make unfavorable comparisons, to prejudge individuals' abilities, and to set inflexible standards for work and careers.

Use the space below to describe experiences that have reinforced traditional female or male priorities and stereotypes in you. Who tried to influence your career choices as a child, in high school, or college? Or after a major transition such as moving, divorce, or marriage, what did parents, teachers, close friends, managers say? What choices did other people close to you make and what did others say about them? Notice how strong the old messages are.

As a child I was influenced to choose a career by:

_____

_____

_____

_____

_____

In school by:

_____

_____

_____

_____

_____

COMMON STEREOTYPES
(Continued)

At work by:

_____

_____

Things I saw or heard in the last few days which relate to the career choice of men and women:

_____

_____

Taken as the whole truth, many of the sex role messages we hear depersonalize us. As psychologist Herb Goldberg says in *The New Male Female Relationship*, stereotypes turn men into insensitive machines and keep women like children. They limit our ability to relate to each other successfully at home and on the job.

At work male and female stereotypes keep us from taking steps which would add to our professional growth and contribute to major career accomplishments. They prevent us from making important contributions to the success of teams and organizations. Narrow views of the other sex cause us to misunderstand them and block their progress.

Fortunately, there is another side to the story. Most of us are capable of going beyond our upbringing and social pressure to bring our best to new roles we play in the workplace. We can learn to talk to ourselves and each other differently. We can help each other to learn this. In the words of Alice Sargent:

Men and women should learn from one another without abandoning successful traits they already possess. Men can learn to be more collaborative and intuitive, yet remain result oriented. Women need not give up being nurturing in order to learn to be comfortable with power and conflict.

The Androgynous Manager, p. 37
by Alice Sargent © 1983 AMACOM, a division of American
Management Association, New York. All rights reserved.

COMMON STEREOTYPES
(Continued)

Use the space below to illustrate one way in which you have broken through the traditional female or male mold and called on the "other side" of your nature to act out of different priorities or discover new ways of thinking. Use words, pictures, or whatever best expresses this breakthough.

Breakthroughs take extra effort because the culture around us and our "self-talk," pull us in other directions. High achieving women often struggle with one such set of messages, the "Cinderella Complex"—the repeated temptation to give up their hard won success for a man.* Men who chose less bottom-line-oriented professions or become househusbands tell how they are plagued by guilt and worry, "Am I a real man?"

If you don't feel like you've made such a breakthrough, use the space to create a picture of how you might like to change and advantages that change might bring to you, your work or your home life.

**Another
side of me**

---

* See the book by this title listed in Task 10.

COMMON STEREOTYPES
(Continued)

Our co-workers and partners may add to the stress of change when they try to keep us from "rocking the boat." A high ranking professional woman noted, "I felt angry about supporting my husband between careers and he felt guilty for not earning the income we were both used to." If we aren't careful we will sabotage and keep each other from reaching our goals.

Herb Goldberg gives us a good discription of the dynamic forces involved as we face the challenge of trying to make non-traditional choices or supporting others who do:

> *. . .the gender undercurrents by which we are pulled along are powerful, complex and immense. Great efforts are needed to recognize, analyze and change them. To understand the gender undertow is to understand the powerful, defensive nature of our conditioning, and to harness a force that is equivalent in a sense to the task and potential of harnessing nuclear energy. Gender undertow is the enormous power of our psyches operating invisibly and powerfully, based on the gender conditioning that creates much of the way we see ourselves as men and women.*
>
> *Herb Goldberg, in The Inner Male*
> pp. xii - xiii

Following are some of the forces which pull at me when I try to break with my traditional role expectations:

FORCES IN FAVOR OF CHANGE   **FORCES AGAINST CHANGE**

THE GOOD NEWS &
THE BAD NEWS

Let's review both the good news and bad news about our situation as women and men in today's workplace. Can you add to the lists below from what you learned in this section?

Good News	Bad News
Men and women are capable of a full range of human behavior.	Powerful forces within us and around us limit our ability to exercise that power.
Biologically and culturally, women and men are given both common and separate strengths.	Individuals are stereotyped as "typical" females or males and not encouraged or given opportunities to develop.
Men and women working together can learn from each other and complement each other in accomplishing their objectives.	Women and men tend to blame each other and avoid what they do not understand about each other.
Organizations have a vast reservoir of energy and creativity in both sexes which can help them be more successful.	Organizations tend to deny problems, supress differences, maintain stereotypes.
I can influence my priorities and stereotypes by how I talk to myself.	Many people will not make the effort because they do not see the possibility of going beyond their stereotypes.
Add other good news:	Add other bad news:
_____	_____
_____	_____
_____	_____
_____	

T A S K 4

SPEAK WITH RESPECT

How we talk to ourselves is critical to how we behave as men and women. Now it is time to look at how we talk to each other. How can we respect and encourage each other as working partners? Will the unspoken language of gestures and emotions be consistent with the words we speak? This section will help you answer these questions.

WE DON'T SPEAK THE SAME LANGUAGE

No doubt you've heard it said, that women and men ''don't speak the same language.'' Here's a quiz which will help you discover some of the ways in which we communicate differently and the effect this has on our working together.

Mark the statements below ☐T rue or ☐F alse.

☐ 1. Men talk more than women do.

☐ 2. Women interrupt men more frequently than men interrupt women.

☐ 3. Men look at women more often when conversing with them than women look at men.

☐ 4. Women learn languages more quickly than men.

☐ 5. In discussions involving both men and women, women tend to set the agenda and determine the topics that will be discussed.

☐ 6. In a mixed discussion, women talk about a wider range of subjects than men do.

☐ 7. In a conversation with another person, a woman generally nods to show that she agrees with the speaker.

☐ 8. Women speak more politely than men.

☐ 9. Men and women use the same set of words.

Now, check your results against the research findings on page 43.

WHEN WORDS OFFEND

No one can accurately predict which words, phrases and ways of speaking will cause discomfort to a particular woman and man. This depends on both the stage of development people find themselves in as well as how the regional and corporate culture speaks the language. Below is a list of ways of speaking which are common offenders in the workplace.

Notice that even here we are different. For the most part men are not offended or put off by the words women use as much as the content or timing of what women say. "Actions speak louder than words," for men.

Ways Men Annoy Women

Calling women *girls,* or addressing women as *sugar, honey, gal, cutie-pie, doll, love, lady, cupcake, etc.*

My wife doesn't work...(outside the home omitted)

Using *guys* in a genderless sense, often mixed with sports metaphors, as, *Okay guys, let's get down to blocking and tackling...*

Physically agressive or violent language and metaphors: *"We have a real blockbuster of a product here and we are going to murder the competition...*

Ways Women Annoy Men

When men want *"straight talk"* (task oriented responses) and they get relationship oriented responses.

Chit-chat, not quickly getting down to business in a business context.

Trying to be *"one of the guys"* by using profanity or telling off-color jokes.

When women say *Tell me your real feelings...*

When a man asks...*and how do you feel about this...?* and actually gets feeling answers in response.

Note the male and female forms of many words are not equivalents and tend to diminish women.
  Master..............Mistress
  Major ....Majorette

To avoid diminishing women, new forms can be used for both sexes and superfluous words can be omitted, e.g. *Flight attendant,* for both *Stewardess and Steward Doctor,* instead of *Lady Doctor*

MALE DOMINANCE

Because of how our society has been shaped over the centuries, it has a large bias in favor of maleness. We call this bias "male dominance." It expresses itself in domination

- over nature and the environment.
- over other men.
- over women.

We are slowly changing our outlook as we realize how this extreme way of looking at things, which people long took to be the "natural order," works against all of us.

- It threatens our survival on the planet Earth by destroying the environment.
- It exploits large numbers of men economically and socially.
- It consistently devalues and exploits women.

This is not to say that "men are no good." Rather, we are now aware that cultural beliefs which benefit some people, deprive others, both women and men, in various parts of their lives. Both sexes have played a role in creating and maintaining this present situation where power, authority, and status are seen as male privileges only sometimes and partially shared with women.

Language is very important in preserving dominance. What men and women say both verbally and nonverbally, and how they say it, can reinforce this imbalance. On the other hand, language can be used to change society from a male-dominant frame of mind to one that works better for all of us today.

Let's look at how language can either make us better partners on the job or divide us and subordinate one sex to the other. We will pay attention both to the spoken word and to the language of gestures and emotions, since we use all three of them to relate to each other.

ANSWERS TO "WE DON'T SPEAK THE SAME LANGUAGE:"

RESEARCH DATA SHOWS:

1. **True.** Men claim more air time than women. They also talk for longer periods at a time and more often than the women in a mixed group. **Result:** Women often withdraw from conversations or talk to each other.

2. **False.** In mixed groups men make 96% of all interruptions, though in single sex groups both men and women interrupt each other equally. **Result:** Women have greater difficulty in presenting their ideas fully. Men feel that women contribute less and fail to benefit from their presence on a team.

3. **False.** Women tend to focus on a speaker, whether male or female more steadily than men do. **Result:** Men perceive women as uncritical listeners or even as flirting; women experience men as arrogant.

4. **True.** Women tend to develop language capabilities sooner then men do. **Result:** Some women are perceived by men as taking advantage of them verbally; some women perceive men as less intelligent or confused.

5. **False.** Men tend to control the topics of conversation. **Result:** Women feel excluded or become bored; men are deprived of opportunities to broaden the range of their interests.

6. **True.** Women will bring up more topics in a mixed discussion than men will. **Result:** Men are seen as fixated on work, sport, etc. while women are seen as flighty or lacking in focus.

7. **False.** Women tend to nod to acknowledge the speaker and indicate that they are listening. Men are more likely to nod only when they want to show the other person that they agree with what is being said. **Result:** Men often presume that women are agreeing with them when in fact they do not. Women see men as disinterested, stubborn, or not listening.

8. **True.** Women use more filler words as well as "women only" adjectives, adverbs, and constructions (It's *just so really wonderful* to see how *nice* everyone looks...) which lighten their speech and make it less intrusive sounding (I hope you wouldn't really mind if...) **Result:** Men don't get the essential message of women's communications, or they don't take women seriously; women feel powerless in certain conversations with men.

9. **False.** Both men and women have words which they use more frequently than the other sex and some words which few people of the other sex ever use. **Result:** We sometimes fail to understand or comprehend each other.

THE LANGUAGE OF EMOTIONS

There are cultural rules about what emotions women and men should have and how they should express them. The illustration below shows the most common traditional (white middle class) messages which we receive about feelings.

In recent years both women and men have made efforts to learn how to express their buried side. Many have succeeded both in making changes with themselves and in training their children. You may be one such person. Still this model will help you to understand reactions when traditional behaviors reassert themselves, or when you must work under stress, or when you collaborate with people with a more traditional outlook.

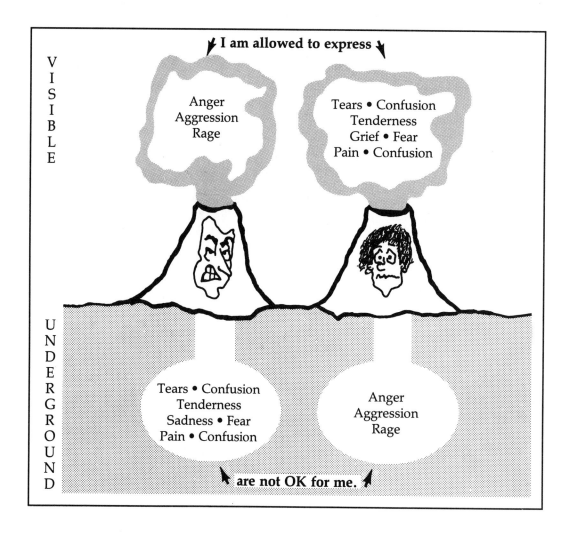

THE LANGUAGE OF EMOTIONS
(Continued)

Like volcanos, our emotional lives have parts that are visible on the surface, which we show to others, and deeply buried, powerful parts, which are "underground." Traditionally, women are almost exactly the opposite in what they show and what they hide because they have been given contrary messages about what is appropriate and what is not allowed.

The underground emotions of men and women tend to express themselves through the side that culture encourages. So:

> **Many men show feelings like sadness, confusion, fear, pain, and even affection through aggressive, angry-looking behavior.**
>
> **Many women, on the other hand, cry, smile, or look confused when they are actually angry about something.**

You will see men who like each other roughhouse or "hit on" each other as a sign of friendship when they get together. A man may yell, "Will somebody tell me what's going on here?" in an irritated tone of voice when he is confused or uncertain. Likewise you will find women who break into tears and walk away from a conversation when things have been said which enrage them.

Here are some *Tips* for dealing with each other's emotions:

> *For Men*
>
> *Women's tears in the workplace are rarely about sadness and loss. When you see a woman looking tearful, rather than moving in to calm, touch, take care of her, or otherwise "fix" the situation; stay where you are, and ask what she wants to say or do. Or ask a leading question like, "If I were in your situation I would be angry. How is it for you?"*
>
> *For Women*
>
> *Men's anger can mean a lot of different things. When a man looks or sounds angry, do not walk away (unless you have solid evidence to believe that the situation is truly dangerous). Instead encourage him to talk more, asking more about what is going on and what he believes is taking place.*

Both women and men can benefit by using the **Ask & Tell** skills which start on page 62.

LANGUAGE THAT INCLUDES EVERYONE

Whenever we listen or read, we must decide whether or not we are personally the subject. In recent years writers, publishers and media experts have set standards by which women, who have a stake in what is being discussed, as well as men can feel included. Here is paragraph which does not include women. It comes from the policies and procedures of a small corporation.

> *If for some reason, a lack of power or hazardous conditions occurs, it is at the discretion of the president, or his representative to close the office. If he decides this, each employee is paid for 7½ hours for that day, regardless of the actual number of hours he has worked.*

As the organization became aware of how language included and excluded people on the basis of sex, the paragraph was rewritten like this.

> *If for some reason, a lack of power or hazardous condition occurs, it is at the discretion of the president, or the president's representative to close the office. If such a decision is made, each employee is paid for 7½ hours for that day, regardless of the actual number of hours worked.*

Here is another paragraph from that same manual before it was revised. Read it over carefully, once as yourself and a second time as if you were of the other sex. Feel the difference.

> *Each new man on the job will pass through a 90 day probationary period during which he can be dismissed if his qualifications do not appear to effectively match his position's requirements. Beyond that he may give or receive in writing a 1 to 4 week notice of separation to terminate the employment relationship. Medical insurance coverage for himself, his wife and family may be applied for immediately.*

LANGUAGE THAT INCLUDES EVERYONE (Continued)

How would you rewrite the section on the facing page to enable both women and men to feel included? Use the space below to create a version that includes all readers.

_____

_____

_____

_____

_____

_____

Choosing the language we use is just as important when we speak as when we write. We know this unconsciously. Notice how the choice of words and topics can suddenly change when you talk with co-workers of the same sex and someone of the other sex suddenly walks into the room? Imagine or replay from memory such a situation and jot down what you or others might be thinking when this happens:

_____

_____

_____

_____

_____

_____

Tip: To catch the difference in male and female language, listen to what a man is saying imagining that a woman is saying it or vice-versa. Note your reaction and your judgments.

UNSPOKEN DOMINANCE

Psychotherapist Lauren Crux, in her paper on ''Patterns of Power and Authority,'' points out that what we do without words can either reinforce traditional roles and stereotypes or break them. Though people from different cultures have different ways of expressing themselves non-verbally (just as they speak different languages) in most workplaces where the white male culture is dominant, you will find the following observations valid.

1. People with more power are permitted to touch those with less.

In business situations, touch more often indicates dominance than intimacy. **Tips:** *Women need to know that they can use touch to communicate power. There is risk to this because some may interpret their actions as sexual or label the user as ''touchy-feely.'' Men should pay attention to what their touching women may mean to others present.*

2. How much space a person takes up can indicate authority or subordinance.

This refers to everything from the size of one's office to how much space your notes and pencils take at the meeting table. **Tips:** *To be more effective with men, a woman should pay attention to the amount of space she assumes and the amount she grants. A man may want to take up less space so as not to give the wrong message at times when he is not intentionally exerting power.*

3. Posture, gesture, body movement, and dress can indicate power.

Open, expansive, and relaxed posture, gesture, and body movement can indicate an attitude of power and authority. Women are traditionally taught to assume postures which cannot be used for power, but which convey subordinance and submission. **Tips:** *When it is important that a woman convey authority or power, she can make her gestures larger and more expansive and adopt a more open posture. Men can become more flexible by being aware of the messages they send with their posture and gestures and by exploring other ways to express themselves.*

UNSPOKEN DOMINANCE
(Continued)

4. **Making and breaking eye contact belongs to the person with more authority.**

Extended eye contact (staring, looking hard or directly, glaring) can indicate a position of power. In most cultures, girls are taught to look away or down more often than boys. From an early age, young women are conditioned to act submissively if they want approval from others. While good eye contact is for both sexes an important part of effective listening, men are taught to use eye contact to exert power and to coerce and charm. **Tip:** *This is a very sensitive set of behaviors. Pay a lot of attention to what you and others do with their eyes, then slowly experiment with changes.*

5. **Whoever talks more, interrupts, initiates, and changes topics is in charge.**

Men talk more and longer than women, and interrupt more. They are more sensitive to whether any given communication succeeds or fails in reaching its goal. Men use language to attack and solve problems. Women support, agree, understand and approve. **Tips:** *Men can dominate less by talking less and by supporting women who are speaking. Women can refuse to be interrupted and deliberately take charge of initiating and changing topics.*

6. **An employee's time is less valuable.**

The person with more power can keep others waiting, but an employee may not keep the boss waiting. Traditionally women have been taught that men's time is to be valued more highly than their own. **Tips:** *Pay attention to when you are kept waiting and what messages this gives. When agendas are being set, respect the value of each person's time and distribute time intensive tasks and support roles (e.g., taking notes or minutes at a meeting) fairly.*

"Learning the unspoken language of power," Crux says, "increases your possibilities. There is nothing wrong with power in itself; there is only something wrong with one person, one gender, one race maintaining it exclusively." In concluding, she observes that isolation is costly and unnecessary. Forming groups to observe, learn about, and practice these tips can be encouraging and fun.

Pay attention to these power factors for a day at work and use the next page to note what you see. See what actions both traditional and recently learned are used by both men and women to exercise power. What other things, e.g., clothing are used to exert power?

WHAT I NOTICED...

ABOUT TASK 4:

_____

_____

_____

_____

_____

_____

_____

_____

_____

_____

_____

_____

_____

_____

_____

_____

_____

_____

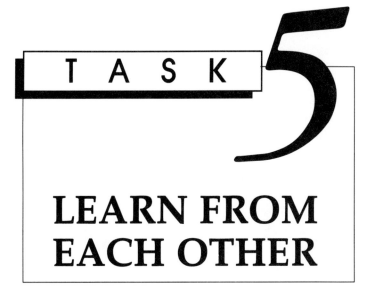

TASK 5

LEARN FROM EACH OTHER

Old stereotypes of what makes a successful worker need to be reexamined along with gender stereotypes. Today what used to be viewed either as male or female skills are both necessary for the success of organizations. What makes both women and men excellent in the workplace? In this section we will examine how to learn useful skills from each other and see what it takes to integrate women and men into creative and productive teams.

WHAT MAKES US EXCELLENT?

Women

Harmony, balance, nurturance, serenity, creativity, and vision are all words used to describe female strengths. What makes women superb? One working woman, a marketing manager pointed out these traits of women at their best:

> *We are able to keep many tasks going at the same time. We can respect, handle and accept when other adults act like children; give insights and criticism without considering the political implications; be honest and loving in giving feedback; balance family and work without letting the family down; work and make decisions intuitively; notice, not make assumptions about what people are saying; include others and be aware of how they see reality when our own view differs.*
>
> *It is not uncommon for a woman to juggle the care of elderly parents, children or other loved ones while giving her all to her job. Care and empathy oftentimes take priority over beating a deadline. A forgiving nature combined with patience and perseverance help her stay steady while tackling problems of great complexity.*

Men

Competitiveness, goal-orientation, tangible accomplishment, problem solving, singleness of purpose, and responsiveness to challenges are attributes often linked to men in our culture. What makes men superb? When asked, one man, a transport engineer answered:

> *Men feel challenged every day to support and protect themselves and their families. This responsibility historically has been met through man's singleness of purpose, loyalty, tenacity, logical ability, physical strength and courage, straightforwardness and sense of what is right.*
>
> *Strong men are seen as focused, professional, able to separate family and work, play politics, work the company strategically, strive with ease toward productivity goals and outputs.*

WHAT MAKES US EXCELLENT?
(Continued)

Think of three of your strengths which traditionally have been considered characteristic of your sex. What are they and how do they contribute to your excellence on the job?

1. _____

2. _____

3. _____

Conventional wisdom tells us that, ''Our greatest strength is also our greatest weakness.'' This is particularly true when we rely on it in the wrong place or at the wrong time and fail to develop other strengths that are more appropriate. ''This is a man's job,'' we say, or ''That's woman's work.'' When Abraham Maslow pointed out that everything looks like a nail to the person whose only tool is a hammer, he could have well been talking about one-sided masculinity or over-played femininity. Learning from each other, women and men acquire more ''tools'' and organizations become more effective when they apply both ''female'' and ''male'' strengths to reach their goals.

Today's workplace is forcing women and men to adopt each other's strong points. Not everyone sees this yet. Have you heard a strong, focused and energetic woman characterized as "pushy" and "demanding?" Or, seen a nurturing and empathetic male characterized as "soft" or "wishy-washy," or called a "wimp?" Most of us have.

What happens in your organization when people step out of characteristic male or female roles? Write your response below.

_____

_____

Today our old roles are becoming blurred both in the workplace and at home. Many functions commonly performed by only one sex are now done regularly by both. Both men and women are expected to be partners at home and teammates on the job. Often both contribute equally to the family economy. Without sharing strengths, this would be impossible. What new expectations have you felt on the job or at home? Write them in the space provided.

_____

_____

WHAT ORGANIZATIONS CAN LEARN FROM WOMEN

The organization of the future asks for a different blend of values. Not only because women are present in larger numbers, but because jobs are changing in the "age of the smart machine." Work requires less muscle and motor skills, and fewer support roles. In the future it will demand even more information, teamwork and person-to-person skills.

Today, women must continue to learn skills that have traditionally been seen as male skills. Men will have to become more proficient at things women have been taught to do. What these are can be seen more clearly by looking at what takes place in organizations which are run largely by women.

Women-run organizations tend to offer a "focus on the individual and personal fulfillment. This results in greater organizational effectiveness and better bottom line results."* In female-dominated organizations there was support for the factors listed below. Check ✔ those whose increase might benefit your organization or you personally.

☐ More emphasis on collaborative decision making.

☐ Less concern with title and formal authority, more concern with responsibility and responsiveness.

☐ Less concern for empire building, power, domination, and consciousness about one's "turf."

☐ A greater concern with process and fairness.

☐ More decentralization.

☐ More democratic, participative, consultative management; less autocratic, domineering, ego-involved management.

☐ More concern with the quality of outcomes.

☐ A greater responsiveness and concern for individual feelings, ideas, opinions, ambitions, and on- and off-the-job satisfactions.

☐ Higher value placed on loyalty, longevity, and interpersonal skills.

☐ More emphasis on skills as a listener and conversationalist.

How does this work in practice? Studies have begun to show that some activities, like negotiation, mediation, and personnel selection are done better by women and men working together rather than individually or in same sex groups.

---

*Adapted from Ginsburg, Sigmund G., "Lessons for American Management from Female Dominated Organizations," *The President*, May 1989

MAKING MIXED TEAMS WORK

Being hired by an organization or appointed to a work group does not mean that you will immediately be accepted as a colleague by the people in it. This is particularly true if you are the only woman or man or one of few in a group made up mostly of the other sex. Below and on the next page are two checklists. Choose the one which is appropriate for you. Rate yourself on each item as follows:

---

3 I do this regularly and comfortably

2 I do this some of the time or with some discomfort

1 I rarely do this or do it with great discomfort.

CHECKLIST #1: When I am in the minority

☐ I ask other members (or past members) of the group, expecially those who have been in the same minority position as I am, to help me understand and deal with specific problems.

☐ When asked for ideas, I do not presume to represent my gender group but speak my opinions as my own, honestly and directly.

☐ I insist on getting my perspectives and values heard, but do not try to impose them on the group.

☐ I realize that my addition to the group may cause discomfort. I make efforts to get to know and deal on an individual and personal basis with members of the group who are uncomfortable with me.

☐ I give others time to get used to me.

☐ I think and speak regularly in terms of ''we'' and ''us,'' as a group, rather than dividing myself from them in terms of ''me'' and ''them.''

☐ I inform and support other members of my sex on the team.

☐ I am willing to learn, respect and play by the rules before presuming to change them.

☐ **Total**

MAKING MIXED TEAMS WORK
(Continued)

CHECKLIST #2: When I am in the majority

☐ I am personally responsive to a new member of the team and actively help him or her "to learn the ropes" and the unwritten rules of the group, without becoming overly protective.

☐ I am careful not to stereotype the minority person or make him or her into a token female or male in the group.

☐ Though I value the perspectives which a person of the other sex brings to the group, I do not ask this person to speak for or represent his or her gender.

☐ I see the addition of someone of the other sex as an opportunity to enrich the abilities of the team and broaden my own perspectives.

☐ I recognize my discomfort with someone different, and am willing to get to know that person on an individual and personal basis.

☐ I make myself think and speak in terms of "we" and "us" when dealing with the minority members of my group and avoid separating the minority from the majority in terms of "us" and "them."

☐ When inclined to make decisions (assignments, promotions) on the basis of "chemistry" or my "comfort zone" with another, I am aware that my unfamiliarity or discomfort with someone's gender may be an unfair criterion for deciding.

☐ I am able to look at a minority group member primarily in terms of her or his contribution, role, or function in the group rather than first as a woman or man.

☐ **Total**

When you have completed either of these quizzes, total your score. A score of 16 or more indicates that you have above average sensitivity and skill in managing minority issues. But don't stop there. Get feedback from others. Does the way they see you square with your self-assessment? Plan how you will improve on the skills in which you got low scores.

CASE STUDIES

On the next three pages are some organizational dilemmas involving men and women. Read each and, in the space provided beneath it, propose your own creative solution to the problem. Consciously employ both female and male strengths as you work on each answer.

Situation 1: For a number of years, the top management team of Megacorp took an annual camping and fishing trip together. When the first woman was added to this team, no one could decide how to handle the situation. They thought of adding spouses to the trip which they had never done previously, but felt that this would change the nature of the event. Finally in frustration they decided to cancel the trip altogether! What are the issues? Can you suggest a more creative solution?

_____

_____

_____

_____

Situation 2: All drivers at the ABC Trucking Company were, until last week, men. On Monday when the first woman hire started, the garage foreman sent her back to the personnel and employment office at headquarters because the garage had no women's restroom. What are the issues? How would you handle it if you were the foreman? If you were the new hire? If you were personnel?

As foreman, I would:

_____

_____

As the new hire, I would:

_____

_____

If I were in personnel, I would:

_____

_____

CASE STUDIES (Continued)

Situation 3: *HiFinance Ltd. is a global enterprise with high management standards. In this year's choice for executive development the obvious front-runner for the two-year Sloan Executive Management Program is a woman who has recently remarried. She is in her mid-thirties and there are rumors that she wants to start a family before it is too late. How do you handle this situation as the executive who is responsible for recommending her? What would you do if you were in the woman's shoes?*

_____

_____

_____

_____

Situation 4: *Alice started on the line and was promoted first to supervisor, then foreman, and finally the second woman manager at Weld-A-Tron. She avoids Julia, the senior woman in the organization who does a lot to help other women move ahead and is branded by male associates as a "single-issue, flaming woman's libber." Alice's women friends in the company now complain that she "walks, talks and dresses like a man." Even worse, she ignores the women down the line. What would you say to Alice if you were one of her friends? If you were Julia? How would you respond if you were Alice?*

_____

_____

_____

_____

Situation 5: *Max Matovich is Marketing Vice-President of Better Than, Inc. He mentors Kate Bonorden, a younger, attractive, very bright middle management woman. Tongues are wagging . . . She seems very close to Max and is on a very fast track. How do you react as Max? As Kate?*

_____

_____

_____

_____

CASE STUDIES (Continued)

Situation 6: *Bill Brass is a hard-driving, demanding, often abrasive executive who was recently promoted to headquarters. Lucy Loyal his executive assistant on the last job was a big part of his success. When Bill departed for the new promotion, Lucy was left behind and is getting "beaten up" by those Bill treated roughly. What should you have done to prevent this if you were Bill? If you were Lucy?*

_____

_____

_____

_____

_____

You can learn more from doing these case studies if you discuss your answers with co-workers of the other sex.

LEARNING CHECK

In this section here's what I learned about myself:

_____

_____

_____

_____

_____

Here's what I learned about women and men working together:

_____

_____

_____

_____

_____

Here's what I need to do to put these learnings into practice:

_____

_____

_____

_____

_____

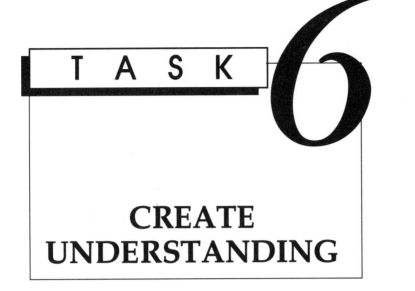

T A S K 6

CREATE UNDERSTANDING

The cultural backgrounds of women and men and the personal experiences of individuals are different, thus we do not automatically hear, think and feel the same things as the result of the words and gestures we use when we talk to each other. It takes special skills to enable us to understand each other well. In this section you will learn and practice these skills.

TWO SETS OF SKILLS

When you are working with someone of the opposite sex or someone of the same sex, for that matter, two sets of skills are critical. They are:

1. Knowing how to understand each other. This means knowing how to **ASK** good questions and **TELL** each other about how we think and feel.

2. Making, keeping, and managing commitments by **TALKING STRAIGHT** with each other.

Traditionally the empathy and concern found in the first set of skills have been women's forte and the second set has been valued in the male tradition. The truth is, most of us, women and men, could be better at both. We are going to look at the first set of skills in this section; the second in the next section.

Understanding each other

There are always three conversations going on when two people are talking with each other. They are numbered in the illustration below. These conversations are always different. Mixing men and women normally increases this difference. There are two sides to every story, a female side and a male side.

When women and men or any two people use the same words, the meanings may be quite different.

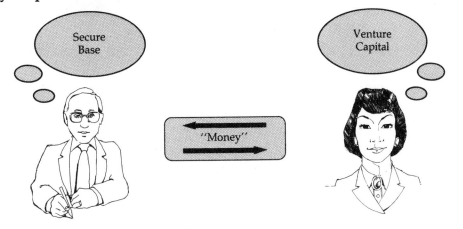

To understand each other, we must exchange enough information to take action and produce the right results. Understanding is always an approximation. We never understand each other perfectly. Breakdowns are always possible for any two individuals, but more likely in situations where men and women are just starting to work together.

Frequently we hear women in the workplace complain about:
- the boss: *He never tells me anything.*
- an employee: *I don't think he listens to me at all.*

While men complain about
- the boss: *She should have known what I wanted.*
- an employee: *I just don't understand how women think.*

To arrive at a better understanding, both women and men must practice **self-disclosure and listening.** In short, they must **ASK** each other the right kind of questions and **TELL** each other what they think, feel, and imagine until they are satisfied that they understand each other well enough to make an agreement.

On the left side of the next two pages are questions which can help you get to know another person's thoughts or feelings. On the right is a list of leading lines you can use to tell the other person about your own thoughts or feelings, even if they do not ask the kinds of helpful questions on the list.

These questions and leading lines enable you to exchange information in a non-threatening and cooperative way. As you practice, you will invent more useful questions and leading lines, but these will help you get started.

TWO SETS OF SKILLS (Continued)

ASK ABOUT	TELL ABOUT

HIDDEN CONVERSATIONS
—WHAT EACH OF YOU IS THINKING OR FEELING BUT NOT SAYING.

What (else) does...mean to you?	*I (also) hear myself saying...*
What do you tell/ask yourself about...?	*I ask/tell myself...*
How do you feel about...?	*I feel... I have a sense that...*
How would you define/picture...?	*Here's how I imagine/feel/define...*
What evaluations are you making about...?	*I've been judging it as...*
	I have a gut feeling that...

*You can use these **basic questions** and leading lines over and over again in the course of the same conversation to arrive at fuller understanding. In conflicts or when you are trying to reach agreement on a course of action, it will be helpful to continue to **ASK** AND **TELL** about the categories below.*

EVENTS—WHAT'S HAPPENING, GOING TO HAPPEN?

Has something happened to bring this about?	*Here's what's happened that leads me to...*
What's going on for you now?	*What's taking place for me now is...*
What do you foresee/hope/fear might happen?	*What I foresee/hope/fear might happen is...*
What occurs to you when...happens?	*When...happens, I usually...*

WINDOWS OF OPPORTUNITY
—WHAT COULD COME OUT OF THIS?

What opportunities do you see in...?	*I see the possibility of...*
What could come out of this?	*There's a chance that...*
What (other) changes would you like to make?	*I would like it to be...*
What do you see yourself doing about...?	*I have a dream that...*
	When it comes to...
What do you imagine would happen if...?	*I imagine myself...*
	It ran through my mind that if...then...

ASK ABOUT	TELL ABOUT

FAILURES & OBSTACLES
—WHAT'S MISSING, NOT WORKING?

ASK ABOUT	TELL ABOUT
What problems are you experiencing now?	*Here's what I see myself faced with . . .*
In your view, what (else) is going wrong with . . .?	*What's going wrong or not working for me is . . .*
What do you believe is missing in order to . . .?	*As I see it, I/we need to . . .*
What do you see as standing in the way of . . .?	*I feel blocked by . . .*

COMMITMENTS—WHAT OBLIGATIONS ARE THERE?

ASK ABOUT	TELL ABOUT
What agreements or promises have you made?	*I promised . . .* *I agreed to . . .*
What plans or preparations do you have for . . .?	*Right now I am involved in . . .* *I see myself ready to . . .*
What are your deadlines/limits/debts/constraints?	*Some of my constraints are . . .* *I have already asked for . . .*
To whom are you answerable for . . .?	*I see myself responsible/required to . . .*
What are you working on now?	*I've already started to . . .*

ALTERNATIVES—HOW ELSE COULD WE LOOK AT IT, DO IT?

ASK ABOUT	TELL ABOUT
What are the pros and cons/(dis)advantages of . . .?	*On the other hand, I see these (dis)advantages . . .*
What other solutions do you see for . . .?	*It also occurs to me that . . .* *Maybe we could . . .*
Is that absolutely the only way for . . .?	*Some possible alternatives might be . . .*
Let's/can you brainstorm a bit . . .	*Let me speculate a bit . . .*

REMEMBER TO LISTEN ACTIVELY

As you listen to others, repeat back to them from time to time what you hear. This helps you to pay attention and lets them know you are listening to them.*

*For more information on this, order *The Business of Listening,* using the form in the back of this book.

HOW TO PRACTICE ASK & TELL

On the next page is a list of concepts that often have different meanings for men and women. Interview a person of the other sex and use this list to practice the skills of **ASK & TELL.** If you are working through this book alone, tell your partner you are trying to improve your communication skills and ask them if they would be willing to spend half an hour doing an exercise with you from the book you are reading.

ASK about the words one at a time. Start by using the questions on page 64 about **Inner Conversation,** for example:

*What does **work** mean to you?*
*What else does **work** mean to you (perhaps several times), etc.*

Then continue using as many questions as you can from the list on pages 64 and 65. Or, you may find it easier to use the tear-out sheet at the end of this book.

When you have asked as much as you think you can about a specific word, **TELL** your inner conversations about the same word. Use the lead-in words on the right side of the page. Remember, **TELLING** does not mean arguing. This is not an exercise in finding out who's right, but in finding out how each of you thinks.

Accept what you hear, and share equally. See how long you can talk about each word. If you manage to **ASK & TELL** so much that you complete only a few words from the list, you are doing very well! You don't have to finish the list. Let your curiosity about the other person drive you. Above all, don't behave like a prosecutor badgering the witness or an amateur psychologist trying to fix another person's thinking.

When first doing this exercise, stick exclusively to the questions and leading lines on your **ASK & TELL** list even though they may seem a bit awkward. After you have practiced for a while, you can invent questions and lines of your own which have the same effect.

Use the empty space alongside the words on the list to make notes about interesting differences you discover between the other person's answers and your own.

You may want to try the exercise with a number of people. It's a great way to get to know someone better.

THE LIST

work

success

achievement

independence

power

strength

competition

security

commitment

friendship

anger

support

money

love

play

teamwork

home

image

APPLYING ASK & TELL

The nurses (female) at St. Ann's were upset with the physicians (male) about the operating room schedule. At every committee meeting the nurses got angry with the male doctors whom they felt always demanded preferential treatment. Finally practicing their new skill of ASK & TELL the nurses and doctors discovered that they had different ideas as to what "starting time" meant. The doctors, who focused primarily on their surgical role, thought that starting time was when they scrubbed. The nurses, who tended to look at the range of activities involved in the operation, expected that the physicians would be ready to operate (scrubbed and suited) at starting time.

Using ASK & TELL also clarified expectations and helped to eliminate stereotypes and misunderstandings between the two groups. The conversation shifted to an entirely new level when the chief physician stopped labeling the nurses as too demanding (Stereotype: women = nagging) and the nurses got beyond their feeling that doctors demanded preferential treatment (Stereotype: men = arrogant).

Anger, generated by the conflicting cultural backgrounds and the self-talk of each sex can make conversations unproductive and give people the feeling that everything operates by different standards for men and women.

Where do you suspect that this may be happening in your organization? Look for anger or discontent aimed at one sex by the other.

_____

_____

_____

_____

_____

Try the skills of ASK & TELL when discussing this situation with someone who takes a different position than you.

Tip: You can also use these skills to mediate a conflict if you ASK questions of both sides and get them to TELL each other about their perceptions and feelings.

T A S K 7

COME TO AGREEMENT

Once we have begun to listen to each other and tell each other what we want and what we mean, it becomes possible to make agreements that we can keep. We also learn to manage those which break down. In this section we will learn the rules of direct and unequivocal language which we can apply to everyday situations involving both sexes.

TALKING STRAIGHT

Just as women say the ability to **ASK & TELL** are a big part of what makes them excellent, men at their best characterize themselves as masters of no-nonsense, down-to-earth, **STRAIGHT TALK.**

More realistically, both sexes could improve their use of both sets of skills. Some men are afraid of using straight talk with women for fear of hurting their feelings. Some women don't use straight talk with men for fear of looking ''pushy.''

Many women are quick to complain that men don't make commitments very readily or keep them very well.

> *John and I are a marketing team, but working with him is very frustrating. I can never get specific times from him for our work together. And when I do meet with him, it's like he's forgotten all the plans I thought we had already agreed on earlier. It feels like I'm always starting from scratch and going backwards. It drives me crazy!*

Men contend that women are not direct, that they beat around the bush and assume that men have made commitments where there are none.

> *I wish Andrea would just get down to business. I'm willing to give her what she needs, but she never asks for it. Then, when I least expect it, she is upset with me because of something she thought I ''should have known.'' We go round and round on this and waste even more time trying to find out whose fault it is.*

Situations like the above are common enough for us to suspect that there is a fatal flaw somewhere in the human mind. We are inclined to take what we imagine and make it absolute truth, not only for ourselves, but for others as well. We saw in the last section that often how we understand words and ideas is different. We will now look at how men and women make assumptions about what they expect from each other, instead of clarifying and negotiating what they want from each other. **Expectations are only expectations until we turn them into agreements.**

On the facing page you will see three critical distinctions that we must be familiar with if we are to create agreements that will help us work together.

THREE CRITICAL DISTINCTIONS

1. AN EXPECTATION	*A conversation I have with myself about how another person should behave which I have either not told to her or him or, if I have, he or she has not agreed to it.*

Example: Marge finds one delivery man particularly rude and obnoxious. Although she has not mentioned this to Jake, her co-worker on the dock, she is angry at Jake because he doesn't seem to share her opinion of the delivery man.

2. AN AGREEMENT	*The result of straight talk. The terms are clearly stated, and both of us have agreed to them.*

Example: Genevieve asks Abdullah to meet with her at four o'clock on Tuesday to review the project report he has written. He promises to do so.

3. A MORAL OBLIGATION	*A commitment coming from what we as individuals or as a society believe to be right or wrong or fair. Its purpose is to safeguard the social order and to respect the individual person.*

Example: Chuck defends Marva when he hears co-workers repeating an untrue rumor about her.

Telling the truth and not doing violence to others are commonly seen as moral obligations. Yet, individuals and cultures frequently disagree on specific moral values and how to carry them out in business. As a result, we often have to treat moral obligations like expectations because we're not sure whether others accept our standards. **ASK & TELL** helps us explore each other's values so that we can, where necessary, create explicit agreements about moral obligations.

THREE CRITICAL DISTINCTIONS
(Continued)

Much of the anger which men and women experience (*Why can't he behave like a **real** husband?* or, *When I married her, I expected her to be a **real** wife and mother to our children.*) comes from disappointed expectations. We literally blame the other person for not being the kind of man or woman our mental stereotypes say he or she ought to be and for not acting in ways which our stereotypes say that person should act.

Conflicting expectations on the job become the basis for double standards, resulting in anger on both sides, e.g.:

Expecting women to do what they're told (usually "grunt work") and not ask a lot of questions.	*Expecting women as professionals to understand the language and know the rules of the organization.*

Agreements or commitments result when we give our word after having understood what was being asked of us and its consequences. When expectations or commitments are not met, a breakdown occurs. How we handle the resulting crisis will depend on whether it was caused by a failed expectation or a broken agreement. Following are some tips for handling each kind of breakdown:

A. EXPECTATIONS

1. **When your expectations are not met...**

   - **Tell the other person what your expectations were,** acknowledging the fact that you had an expectation, not an agreement.

     Here's the way I pictured it... I understand that we did not have an agreement.

     I realize that I did not ask you to...

   - **Talk straight to create an agreement if that is in order.**

     Fran, would you do it this way when it is your turn again?

THREE CRITICAL DISTINCTIONS (Continued)

2. **When you did not meet the other person's expectations...**

- **Ask what her or his expectations were.**

  Tell me what you were expecting and what it meant to you.
  What are you saying to yourself that I should be doing?

- **Empathize by acknowledging the other person's viewpoint or feelings.**
  (This does not mean you agree with that person, just that you can
  understand how he or she sees it.)

  I can understand how you might feel that way if you expected...
  I can see that it makes sense from your point of view that...

- **Talk straight to create new agreement if such is in order.**

  That seems good to me, Jean. I promise to do it Monday night.
  I refuse, Chris, to do that, (but I offer to...)

List some common expectations women have of men and vice-versa.

Women expect men to:

_____

_____

_____

Men expect women to:

_____

_____

_____

B. COMMITMENTS

1. **If you have broken a commitment (or failed in a moral obligation)...**

- **Apologize**

  I apologize, Lonnie, for arriving an hour later than I promised. I know how much
  you wanted to go to lunch before the meeting.

  I ask your pardon, Kim, for not telling you the entire truth about Ronnie. I regret
  the embarrassment that you experienced.

- **Don't make Excuses!**

  Excuses   *I'm sorry, but the traffic was terrible...*

  I just didn't think I could tell you...

''I'm sorry,'' is an excuse, not an apology.

THREE CRITICAL DISTINCTIONS (Continued)

Excuses diminish our power and credibility. As one executive put it, "If I really trust you, you don't break many agreements. If you do break one, I take it for granted that you had a good reason, so I don't need to hear about it. Unless you need something from me to prevent another breakdown later, a simple apology will do."

Don't apologize if you have not broken a commitment!

2. **When the other person has broken a commitment (or failed a moral obligation)...**

Complain

(I have a complaint.) We had an agreement that you would have the job done on Friday. You have not kept that agreement...

You asked for [state terms of agreement] e.g.] me to recruit four volunteers. But now [state the breakdown] you're telling me you don't want them.

You told me... But the facts are...

Complaining is simply stating that a breakdown has taken place. It does not mean "griping" or "nagging." We are concerned with repairing the situation and making solid agreements so that we can work well together. We are not trying to put down or punish the other person, although there may be some unpleasant consequences when a commitment is broken.

- **Ask and tell about inner conversations.**

  How did you understand our agreement?

  Here's what it sounded like to me when you said...

- **Talk straight in order to create a new agreement when necessary.**

  I ask you, Carl, to fulfill your promise now.

  I request, Mary, that we come to a new agreement that... If you keep/break this commitment, I promise to... [state consequences].

  I accept your apology, Terry, for...

  I insist that you take steps to keep this from happening again.

Important: By accepting an apology you agree no longer to deal with the one who made it as if the breakdown still exists.

TALK STRAIGHT

Many people ask, "How can I be more assertive on the job?" The answer lies in **STRAIGHT TALK.** This is your ability to say what you mean and put yourself solidly behind your word, without hesitation, coloring the facts or excuses. As women and men, we know that our minds work differently! We're not sure about what we're saying "yes" to, or we are afraid of hidden expectations. So, we are often reluctant to make commitments, or make them in vague and "iffy" language, leaving ourselves room to blame the other person if something goes wrong. This is why **ASK & TELL** and **STRAIGHT TALK** are both needed to make good agreements.

Following are some examples of **STRAIGHT TALK** at work. Experiment with them as models for talking to each other. You may choose to use words that are less formal, but your intention must be as firm as that in the examples below.

A. Creating Agreement about Action
Straight talk about action is **specific** about what is to be done and when it is to be done. It asks for agreement.

ASK only for what you truly want, but persist in getting it.

I ask you, Nora, to be my partner in this presentation. You will have to review this material before our Thursday morning meeting, then dress for business, and be at the client's office at eight in the morning on Friday. Do you agree to that?

Paul, I'd like to play racquetball with you at ten on Monday morning. Do you accept?

PROMISE only what you will do and keep your word.

I promise, Rita, to pick up the brochures at the printer's tomorrow morning on my way to work.

I accept, Jon, your offer to exchange our office duties on Saturday. I promise to do the report if you will meet the new client. Will that meet your needs?

B. Gaining Agreement about Facts
Straight talk about facts implies that you have and can provide **EVIDENCE** for what you say.

I know, Al, that the new calendar cost $14.06. Here is the receipt.

I believe, Frank, that the keys are on the filing cabinet. I put them there last night and saw them there this morning.

Here's my proposal and the data to back it up.

TALK STRAIGHT (Continued)

C. Defining Terms, Setting Goals & Challenges

This means setting goals and standards which are in line with the career or organizational vision we made for ourselves. If Straight Talk about facts could be described as ''telling it like it is,'' Straight Talk about goals is using your personal or positional authority to, ''tell it like it's going to be.'' Straight talk about goals enables us to talk straight about actions.

I am committed, Hal, to having a business of my own next year.

Our staff, Trudi, is going to have multicultural training before we go overseas.

From now on, during the night shift, there will be three interns on duty in the Emergency Ward at all times.

This is our sales target for July. . .

Whether you are a woman or a man, using **STRAIGHT TALK** in combination with **ASK & TELL** will make you a more powerful, well-rounded person and increase your respect for and ability to work with the other sex.

———————————————●———————————————

What I Have Learned

Test yourself on what you have learned in this section by doing the following exercises:

Use Straight Talk to ask a co-worker of the other sex for something you have been reluctant to speak about until now.

_____

_____

_____

Use Straight Talk to agree to give a co-worker of the other sex feedback about his or her collaboration with you.

_____

_____

_____

WHAT I HAVE LEARNED (Continued)

Use Straight Talk about facts to tell a co-worker of the other sex why it is important for women and men to talk straight to each other on the job.

_____

_____

_____

_____

_____

Use Straight Talk about goals to tell a work partner of the other sex what you are committed to doing to improve understanding between the sexes on the job.

_____

_____

_____

_____

_____

Imagine that a trusted employee who reports to you has failed to turn in a critical report on deadline and seems to be avoiding you. Complain about this to them.

_____

_____

_____

_____

Take the role of the same employee. The deadline was never announced to you. Deal with your boss' expectation without excuses or apologies.

_____

_____

_____

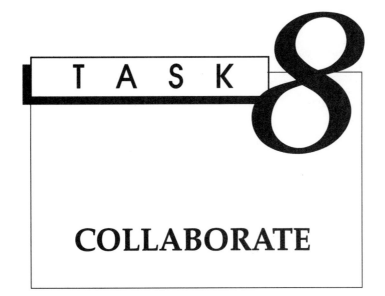

TASK *8*

COLLABORATE

In this section you will learn how, both as boss and employee, to address specific gender issues which affect your work and the work of others. Looking both at the man's point-of-view and the woman's perspective will enable you to collaborate with each other more productively.

WHEN MEN MANAGE WOMEN

Here are some items that men should be wary of when managing women and some tips for how to avoid them.

1. Male Language

Sports and military service provide men with a common vocabulary. Men use sports metaphors like, "When in doubt, punt," "It's time for a full court press," or, "You be our point man." They engage in "strategic" planning, and, when times get tough, "go to the wall," or "bite the bullet." Women can find these terms unfamiliar or even alien to their values. They may misunderstand them and sometimes resent them. *Tip: Take care to explain words which might be unfamiliar. Pay attention to the different ways in which women think and the words they use. Look for new metaphors that both sexes understand.*

Obscene words are also more common in male culture, especially in some workplaces. They are sometimes used deliberately to make women feel out of place. *Tip: Don't apologize for using coarse language in front of women or with women. You would probably be more articulate if you avoided coarse language entirely, but the point here is not to single out women and make an exception of them should you talk this way. Provide leadership for other men in using appropriate and understandable language with women.*

What common "man's world" words are used in your organization? Jot down two of them here and then translate them into a form that both women and men can more easily understand.

_____ **=** _____

_____ **=** _____

2. Male Culture

When entering the workplace, many women find themselves forced to function in a culture made by men. It may not value them highly. They are shunted off to helping roles and given less responsibility and pay than their male counterparts. They are thought of as temporary and not given the information they need to succeed. *Tip: Be aware of any ways in which you "hold back" when dealing with women and how this holds women back by not giving them information, resources, feedback, and responsibility. Note them below.*

_____

_____

WHEN MEN MANAGE WOMEN
(Continued)

3. The Spokeswoman

It isn't fair to make a woman speak for other women just because she is a woman. *Tip: If an issue about women or gender comes up, instead of saying something like "Well, Jane, how do you think the women will react to this?" simply ask, "Who has an opinion on this? Bill? Jane?"*

What other ways of singling out women have you observed on the job?

_____

_____

_____

_____

_____

4. How Women Relate

Some women succeed in an organization, adopt male standards. They behave, talk and "go it alone" like many men do. Other equally qualified, ambitious women decide not to do this. You may work with both types of women. *Tip: Remember, a woman is not necessarily stronger because she acts like a male, or weaker if she looks more feminine or seeks support from other women on a regular basis. Men tend to seek support or work in teams only during a crisis. You may learn a new kind of teamwork from how women network with each other.*

What differences do you notice in how women and men relate to their own sex?

_____

_____

_____

_____

WHEN MEN MANAGE WOMEN
(Continued)

5. Other Kinds of Diversity

Different ethnic and cultural differences may also affect the values and actions of women you work with. Black women, for instance, may appear more independent and thus more threatening to co-workers and managers than non-black women. *Tip: Become aware of how women and men relate to each other in the different cultural groups which exist in your workplace.* Working Together,* *another book in this series may help you.*

What other differences in culture and background affect how women and men behave toward each other in your organization?

_____   _____

_____   _____

6. The Rules of the Game

In predominently male organizations, women may complain that they don't know the procedures or rules, or don't understand them though you may think that the rules are obvious. *Tip: When women ask questions about things that you take for granted, or complain that they are confused or lost in the system, don't assume that they are stupid or playing a game. Believe them. Respond to their need with information and direction.*

One thing women find hard to understand in this organization is:

_____

7. You are taken at your word

Women may be more likely than their male colleagues to take men at their word, literally. A woman may take what you say more seriously than you mean to be taken. *Tip: Be careful to say what you mean, and be clear about what you are committed to when supervising women on the job. Talk straight. Otherwise women will think of you as dishonest or unreliable.*

Make a mark to show how credible you believe you are with women in your organization. Check your answer with others.

LOW CREDIBILITY ‖‖‖‖‖‖‖‖‖‖‖‖‖‖‖‖‖‖‖ HIGH CREDIBILITY

_____

* This title may be ordered using the information in the back of this book.

8. Conflict

Many women are brought up to believe that conflict, particularly conflict with someone in authority, is wrong. Many women have speech patterns that invite others to be included or add comments. They will use words which make them sound less assertive (*only, just, maybe,* etc.), end their sentences with a questioning tone or actually tag on small questions to statements they wish to make (e.g., *Don't you think..., ...isn't it?* etc.). These speech patterns will invite men to interrupt women, to dominate the conversation, or not be aware of how strong a woman's concern, need or demand may be. ***Tip:*** *Be alert to possible sources of conflict and work hard to make sure all sides are heard. If a male team member pushes something through, he may get far less commitment and performance from female teammates than he expects.*

In many organizations, men are rewarded for being *rebels* while women who do this are looked on as *troublemakers.* What is the situation in your organization? Answer the question below. Then check out the feelings of several women you work with on this subject.

_____

_____

_____

_____

_____

WHEN MY BOSS IS A MAN

Here are three things a woman should pay attention to when her boss is a man or she is working in a largely male environment.

1. The over-protective boss

At an early age, men are taught to be careful around women and to protect them. As a result, some men will show a great deal of respect around women and will be committed to helping them succeed. Yet his protectiveness can make you look weak, vulnerable, and childish in other men's eyes and lead them to deal with you as incompetent or in a non-professional way.

For example, your boss or mentor, though he would never consciously patronize you, might, in introducing you, put an arm on your shoulder, or his hand on you. He wants to give the message that he really approves of and supports you, but the action itself makes you look smaller or less capable.

*How to handle it: Tell him you understand and are grateful for his support and concern, but are uncomfortable when it is expressed in certain ways. Show him what he can do differently to send the right message. If he is truly behind you, he will be eager to know how to support you in ways that work best. Be patient but persistent—you are dealing with deeply ingrained feelings and behaviors.**

If you choose a male mentor, pick a man who wants to genuinely bring you along, not one who wants to be a hero or look good by having you work for him and "taking care" of you. Ask for line management with profit and loss responsibility if you find yourself always in staff positions.

On a scale of 1 to 10, My boss supports me:

Too little				**Just Right**				**Over-protectively**
1 —— 2 —— 3 —— 4 —— 5 —— 6 —— 7 —— 8 —— 9 —— 10								

---

*See the tipsheet, "How to Deal with a Sexist Boss" in the Resources Section.

WHEN MY BOSS IS A MAN
(Continued)

2. Feedback

Men will sometimes try to spare women painful feedback. This is a dangerous situation. The boss who tries to be overly nice to you may withhold information that you need to succeed and to do a better job.

How to handle it: Insist on feedback. If he seems reluctant, tell him how important it is for you to get clear and timely feedback that you can act on. Do this now, not at the end of a year or a long appraisal period. Insist on feedback that you can measure against a fixed standard, e.g., ''once every two weeks,'' or ''in terms of my performance goals.''

Here is one area of my work in which I could benefit from more specific feedback:

_____

_____

_____

3. Self-Disclosure

Be somewhat cautious about how openly you discuss personal issues. Men may misread your intentions when you share your feelings, express family needs and priorities, or react emotionally to events occurring in the organization. They may read you as weak or uncommitted, or fear being implicated in matters that make them uncomfortable. They will see you as a misfit, attempt to deal with you as a misfit rather than seeing how the structure and attitudes of the organization may be making it hard for women to succeed.

How to handle it. Make sure what you disclose is put in straightforward, matter-of-fact terms which are related to the tasks of your job and the goals of the organization.

Here is one personal concern I feel strongly about, that affects my productivity on the job.

_____

_____

_____

WHEN WOMEN MANAGE MEN

Here are some of the difficulties which women may experience when managing men and some tips to handle them.

1. Machismo

For some men, answering to a woman as manager, or as team-leader, is a severe blow to their ego. They may feel anxiety, energy, shame or guilt. *Tip: There is not a lot you can directly do to change such feelings and judgments because they are deeply rooted in the culture of the individual. Above all avoid trying to argue with these men—your authority is not negotiable. Men who respect you will be your allies in dealing with such persons. If you are the first woman manager and your entire group seems to behave in this way, you have a tough challenge, but firmness, consistency, and fairness in what you ask or demand will be the best tools for dealing with the situation.*

2. Holding a "Man's" Job

Men sometimes complain that a woman holds her job only *because* she is female; either implying that she is an affirmative action appointee, or worse that she owes her position to currying favor with a man in power. This may be a "sour-grapes" reaction if the woman was competing with a man to get the job. *Tip: Remember that in competing with a man for a project or promotion, you compete with his self-image as a man. Men tend to identify with their work more than with anything else. Losing a promotion to a woman is likely to be more humiliating than losing to another man. Your competence will demonstrate your legitimacy.*

Both issues have to do with men accepting your authority. You will want to move as quickly as possible from being seen as one who exercises authority only by virtue of the position she holds, to being one whose authority is based on the ability to inspire and influence others.

Check ✔ the categories of skills which would help you become a more authoritative and influential person.

	Effective Presentation		**Team Building**
	Negotiation		**Coaching & Counseling**
	Influencing Others Face-to-Face		**Making Humor Work**

Note: Several of the Fifty-Minute Books listed in the back of this book can help you sharpen these skills.

WHEN WOMEN MANAGE MEN
(Continued)

3. Men Tough it Out

Men are even less likely to ask for help in a task from a woman manager than they are from other men. This means that your male subordinate may be inclined to go it alone when he most needs help. *Tip: Be alert for cues which indicate that he is overextended or in trouble. Keep a close eye on deadlines and outputs. Stay in touch and offer help in a matter of fact way when the stress is high.*

4. Giving Directions

Men like to look like they know what they are doing and where they are going. Women complain, for example, that some male drivers when lost are reluctant to ask for directions. One woman found it humorous that, ''When he finally decides to ask for directions at a gas station, he manages to turn the car around so that I am closest to the attendant and I get the job of asking for directions.'' Likewise, on the job some men fail to ask questions when they need to know something and mask their confusion and uncertainty with a self-assured look *Tip: Monitor carefully what is going on. Don't leave such a man without information he needs or overload him and not know about it.*

5. Anger and Irritation

Men are trained by their culture to go on the offensive when they feel vulnerable. Therefore doubts, fears, insecurities, and disappointments are likely to be expressed in angry words and gestures. *Tip: Try to look beneath the external expression, to the situation which he is responding to, if you want to understand his feeling in your own terms. Use the skills of asking and listening to do this.*

Some of the clues which tell me when a man is in trouble or in need of direction are:

- ☐ He is irritable.

- ☐ He avoids me.

- ☐ He blames me.

- ☐ He brings up related issues on a ''what if. . .'' basis.

- ☐ _____

WHEN WOMEN MANAGE MEN
(Continued)

6. Many Masculinities

If you are working in an environment where there are a variety of men from different cultures and backgrounds, don't be surprised if they react to and treat you differently. *Tip: Learn something about their standards and teach them yours.* Working Together, *another book in this series will show you how to deal with this added dimension.*

Other cultural differences besides gender which come into play with the men who work with me.

☐ AGE   ☐ TECHNICAL BACKGROUND

☐ RACE   ☐ _____

☐ EDUCATION   ☐ _____

WHEN MY BOSS IS A WOMAN (FOR MEN)

Here are some of the things a man should be careful of when interacting with a female boss or working in a strongly female environment.

1. Mother or Teacher

Many men unconsciously look at their boss as if she were their mother or teacher. This is not meant to corroborate the common complaint that many men are "fixated on their mothers." It is simply a fact that the only models of women with authority that many men have experienced were at home or in school. In some organizations a female boss is actually called "Mom," or, "Teach." *Tip: If you find yourself complaining a lot to your female boss, or confiding your personal problems to her; or, on the other hand, if you act consistently rebellious toward her, you might be acting out of unconscious images of women in authority. Ask yourself, "If she were a man, would I behave this way?"*

How would I deal with me if I were her?

_____

_____

_____

WHEN MY BOSS IS A WOMAN
(Continued)

If you have not had sisters or close non-sexual friendships with other women, you may also run the risk of casting a woman boss or co-worker in an unconscious "girlfriend" role. *Tip: You could hurt your working relationship and even your career by playing either the "priest" or the "playboy." On one hand keeping her at a deliberate distance or treating her coldly so as not to become involved emotionally or physically; or, on the other hand becoming too familiar or intimate.*

When dealing with women in authority my tendency is to be:

Too intimate   Just right   Too distant

|———|———|———|———|———|———|———|———|———|

3. Being too careful

If you are uncomfortable with a woman boss or co-worker, you might inform her less than you would a man. As a result she will begin to see you as secretive, devious, or not trustworthy. This could cost you efficiency on the job and hinder your career. Women bosses often complain that men try to be too careful around them and that this infuriates them. *Tip: To avoid "walking on eggs" in the presence of a strong woman, be open, direct, and ask questions. Putting yourself in her shoes is probably your best tool for understanding both yourself and her position.*

Issues I am likely to avoid when dealing with a woman in authority:

_____

_____

_____

_____

_____

HOW TO SUPERVISE PEOPLE IN GENDER CONFLICT

As a manager of either sex, you may be called upon to deal with hostility between women and men. The following checklist will tell you if you are ready to mediate a conflict over gender issues. Check ✔ the items that are true of you.

☐ **I am fully informed** and clear about my organization's stand on gender issues. I know personnel policies and procedures concerning hiring, promotion, sexual harassment, as well as the company philosophy and the working climate.

☐ **I am clear about what I stand for and believe.** I am alert to old values which may be at odds with my present commitment to fairness and understanding.

☐ **I do not become political** or take sides on feminist issues or men's rights. When dealing with others conflicts, I see that my job is to create a situation in which two people can work together more productively, not to make one party right and the other wrong.

☐ **I facilitate and inform.** I help the parties to listen to each other by listening well myself. I am direct and clear with them about how I and my organization are committed to the resolution of gender issues.

☐ **I am aware of my legal obligations** to act in certain ways, for example in cases of sexual harassment. I stay up to date on the law and know where to go for counsel when I am unsure of what to do. I am able to advise others about their rights and responsibilities.

☐ **I remain as fair and impartial as possible.** I neither bend over backwards to avoid being seen as favoring my own sex nor do I cave in to those who try to play on my sympathies and use the fact that we are both of the same sex to get me to back their position.

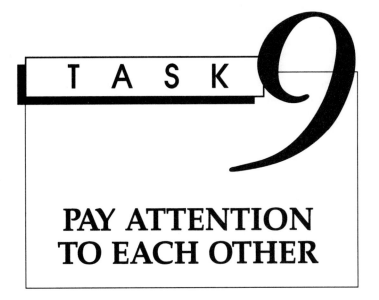

TASK 9

PAY ATTENTION TO EACH OTHER

To become partners in the organization of the future will take vision, fresh attitudes and skills. Along the way we will have to recognize and encourage each other as well as learn from others and teach them what we know. This section helps you formulate and begin work on these goals as well as deal with relationship pitfalls which can occur along the way.

GETTING A VISION

By this point you should be aware that for women and men to become creative partners takes effort and skill. To sustain ourselves we need a compelling vision, new beliefs, and the ability to encourage each other day after day. Picture in your mind a brighter future for men and women. What would it look like? Describe it vividly in words or images below.

Build the Mental Framework

To support your vision, you can begin by talking to yourself in new ways, replacing old stereotypes and expectations with new, more positive affirmations. Write some of the things you can say to yourself that will encourage you to persist in bringing about your dream.

I believe _____

I can _____

I am committed to _____

RECOGNIZING EACH OTHER

Traditionally women are recognized and rewarded for certain traits and behaviors and men for others. This trains us to be feminine or masculine. It makes us feel good when we do the things that ''real'' women and ''real'' men do. On the other hand we also want to be recognized when we try out new roles and behave in new ways.

List a few of the things which you would like others to recognize about you.

The kind of man or woman I am	Breakthroughs I have made

Because women and men bring separate strengths to their collaboration with each other, and because they can improve their teamwork and performance by learning from each other, it is important to give each other both **enough recognition** and **the right kind of recognition.**

Enough recognition.

Recognition is the most powerful tool we possess to energize and motivate individuals as well as to mold them into a working team. Organizations where people are recognized have power, skills, and depth in their human resources. Do men and women where you work give each other enough recognition?

RECOGNIZING EACH OTHER
(Continued)

Cross out the words in the following exercise that do not relate to you:

Personally, I receive | *too little • just enough • too much* | *recognition from others.*

I feel that people | *do • do not* | *recognize me for the right things.*

Most of the time I | *do • do not* | *know where I stand with others.*

In my organization people give others | *less • about the right amount • more* | *recognition than they deserve.*

| *Men • women* | *are given more recognition than* | *women • men* | *where I work.*

Acknowledging a woman at work, for her appearance and for traditional ''feminine'' virtues like patience and gentleness, may feel good to her, but it can also seem like a conspiracy to keep her in her place if that's the only recognition she gets. She needs to know that others appreciate how she does her job as an individual and how she contributes to her team's accomplishments.

Women complain that men have boundless egos. While it is true that men who have been forced to be competitors need a lot of reassurance; they also need support and recognition for trying things that are new and different and perhaps less ''masculine.''

Many men and women are reluctant to recognize each other. They are afraid they will lose something if they applaud someone else. Men, who take each other for granted, balk at giving women special credit for accomplishments. Women, on the other hand, may hesitate to acknowledge men for traditional ''male'' behaviors for fear that they will reinforce the ''machismo'' which is often used ''to keep women in their place.''

Some men hesitate to affirm women in ''old fashioned'' ways i.e., for their attractiveness or other ''female'' qualities, afraid that liberated women will find this offensive or see it as ''buttering them up.'' Women may be reluctant to applaud men for their accomplishments and risks because they feel men already have all the advantages.

Such thinking creates a great **shortage of recognition** in the workplace. We continually hear about what people don't like and what we do wrong, but give each other very little support and encouragement.

RECOGNIZING EACH OTHER
(Continued)

Do you feel hesitant to recognize individuals of the other sex, or of your own sex? What do you tell yourself about this?

_____

_____

_____

_____

_____

The right kind of recognition.

Some of these forms of recognition are less than an acknowledgement. Let's examine several:

1. Flattery

The flatterer gives people compliments or acknowledgement _to get something for themselves._ Flattery is exaggerated or insincere praise. It's used to get others to give us something we want or to charm them into liking us or to take our side. Most of us, of course, expect that acknowledging others will result in better relationships and improved teamwork—mutual benefits to both of us. But flattery goes much further. The flatterer benefits _at the expense of_ the person being flattered.

> _Mark goes out of his way to tell Lois that she is doing a great job. He knows that she is moving to a similar position in the accounting department in a month and does not want to go through the effort of training her since he believes she is a slow learner._

2. Compliments

Compliments are common courtesies. Most of us enjoy positive strokes from others. We use exclamations like, "Good show!" "Nice work!" "You look great today!" accompanied by a smile, a handshake, or a pat on th back. Compliments make working with others more enjoyable. Usually they are partial acknowledgements rather than full recognition, however. Sometimes they are just politeness—a very mild form of flattery, or expressions of our own tastes, preferences and values.

THE RIGHT KIND OF RECOGNITION (Continued)

Even when they are sincere, compliments carry with them an unspoken level, the message that *the giver is somehow superior to* the person he or she compliments.

> *"You're really coming along,"* Harriet tells Bob when he returns to the office to tell *her of the deal he closed. Harriet believes the best way to manage her sales staff is to give them little pats on the back as often as she can.*

3. Full Recognition

When you fully recognize someone you are really declaring to them (and to others who hear it) that you see and recognize what they have achieved, accomplished or done, and you want them (and often others) to know it.

> *I congratulate you Chris! You've sold our toughest customer and did it in record time.*
>
> *I want everyone to know, Pat, that you were the one who led the team that put our new product into production ahead of schedule.*
>
> *I respect you, Dale, for giving everyone a chance to air their opinion.*

Notice that these examples have some things in common.
1. The speaker talks in the **first person.**

I congratulate you...   I respect you...

Say **"I."** You can recognize a person with a simple, *"Thanks for...,"* or *Congratulations!"* but speaking for yourself is more powerful.

2. The speaker uses a **direct language which does what it says.**

I respect you, Dale...   I congratulate you, Chris...

You can broaden your vocabulary of acknowledgment to fit a variety of situations by employing such phrases as:

I recognize you for...	*I am proud of you because...*
I respect you for...	*I applaud you for...*
I compliment you on...	*I give you credit for...*
I appreciate the fact that you...	

THE RIGHT KIND OF
RECOGNITION (Continued)

3. The speaker uses the other person's **personal name** not nicknames, or feminine diminutives like *Honey, Dear, Dearie,* or machoisms like, *Buddy, Big Fella', Pal, etc.*

> *I respect you,* **Dale**...   *I congratulate you,* **Chris**...

4. The speaker is **specific** about what the other person has done or accomplished. Remember when recognizing a woman, point to what she has achieved rather than to good looks, patience, or some other submissive virtue.

The more detail you include, the more you are telling the person that you have really noticed what he or she has done. It's especially gratifying when you reflect the other person's feelings about the accomplishment, not just the benefit it has brought you or the organization. Here are a couple of good examples:

I give you credit, Jill, for attending and completing the economics night study program at City College. I know how much you wanted to succeed in that field.

I am grateful to you, Jack, for organizing our travel plans and making all the reservations in advance for the convention. We would never have been able to do all we did if you hadn't put so much time into it—it must have been hard work.

The language of these four steps may at first seem awkward, but once you see how powerful acknowledgement can be, it will become second nature to you. On the next page there is space to practice acknowledgment in writing. You might want to start, however, by thanking the person who told you about this book or acknowledging someone who has practiced some of these exercises with you.

PRACTICE ACKNOWLEDGMENT

In the space below, acknowledge people with whom you work. Make sure you get the four elements of full recognition in each.

Full recognition for someone of the other sex

I _____ you _____
        (Acknowledgment Words)   (Personal Name)

for _____
                            (Specific Accomplishment)

_____

_____

Full recognition for someone of the same sex

I _____ you _____
        (Acknowledgment Words)   (Personal Name)

for _____
                            (Specific Accomplishment)

_____

_____

Recognition for myself.

I _____ you _____
        (Acknowledgment Words)   (Personal Name)

for _____
                            (Specific Accomplishment)

_____

_____

R℞ *Habit forming. Using recognition three times a day until it becomes a regular and normal behavior will remedy much tension between women and men in the workplace. You cannot overdose.*

WHEN WORK IS SEXY

Let's face it—work is sexy. Put men and women together in the workplace and it is impossible for there not to be some sexual dynamics at play. Where work is monotonous and tedious, the interplay of the sexes provides variety and stimulation. On the other hand, where peak performers are doing what they love, it is easy for the synergy and excitement to take on sexual overtones.

What can a manager do to deal with an employee who flirts with co-workers?

Some flirting can ease sexual tensions in a work group. It playfully acknowledges the sexual dynamics between women and men and keeps them from becoming disruptive. It may serve as a safety valve for people who need to recognize but not act on sexual attraction in the workplace. On the other hand, excessive or unwanted flirting and flirting done in poor taste may unnecessarily raise sexual tension and cause antagonism.

When flirting becomes one-sided or demeaning, give people feedback about their behavior and the productivity problems it causes. Be clear and direct about how you expect people to behave on the job. If necessary, state what the consequences will be if the disruption continues.

How should you handle workplace romance?

Workplace romance has both positive and negative consequences.

People can become more creative, and productive, have higher morale and become better team players. Particularly where people have demanding careers and work long hours, affection and romance can make the difference between excitement and energy and loneliness and depression. The risks and frustrations of casual liaisons are reduced.

Organizations fear office romances because they threaten to disrupt the lines of authority and the productivity of the people involved and those around them. Many relationships carry with them the potential of adverse publicity, especially when they involve corporate "higher-ups" or people already in committed relationships with others.

WHEN WORK IS SEXY (Continued)

Romance can occur at any level of an organization. Some people have few opportunities outside work in which to search for romance and partnership.

Try as you will, the chances are very poor of keeping office romances secret. There are subtleties which people pick up and soon everybody knows and is talking. As a result, co-workers start dealing with the ''couple'' differently. They become afraid to share information with one or the other, etc.

Most organizations have rules about romantic relationships. Guidelines may be spelled out in policies and procedures, or there may be unwritten rules which the unknowing discovers only through painful experience. Few organizations encourage the growth of romantic relationships, but some have a *laissez-faire* attitude—anything goes. In many organizations, romantic or sexual relationships are not spoken about, but people who engage in them quickly run into animosity from others.

Whether you are a manager dealing with someone else's workplace romance, or you yourself become involved in an intimate relationship, you should know the risks. If the rules are not spelled out, pay attention to the stories people tell and how openly they relate to each other as men and women.

The following checklist provides things a manager can do to deal with workplace romance. Check ✔ those you think you can do well. Put a zero **0** before those for which you need to do some homework.

☐ I can tell the difference between romance which is consented to by both parties at each step in its development, versus one-sided behavior which may constitute sexual harassment.

☐ I know what the rules, policies and procedures of the organization say about such relationships.

☐ I also know the unwritten rules and norms of the company culture.

☐ I face the situation at the outset and am willing to talk about it with those involved. I avoid trying to look like I do not see what is taking place, or try to keep it hidden.

WHEN WORK IS SEXY (Continued)

☐ I help people see clearly what their situation looks like to outsiders and explain what the choices and consequences of their behavior might be.

☐ When a couple is inclined to deny what is happening (even though it shows in their behavior and work), I encourage them to accept the possibility of attraction or romance and take responsibility for managing it.

☐ If the relationship is disrupting work, I avoid personal judgments about the people involved, but clearly point out to them the effects that it has or may have on productivity, authority, their careers, etc.

☐ I keep my own discomfort under control and continue to communicate with and listen to both parties with fairness, empathy and candor.

TIPS FOR OFFICE ROMANTICS

Here is a checklist drawn in part from tips given by authors Lisa Maniero and Leslie Westoff for successfully managing matters of the heart in the workplace (**USA Today,** Aug. 7, 1989). Mark **Yes** or **No** in the columns at the right. If both of you can say yes to each of these items, you have the best chances of making your romance work and getting your work done.

Conditions for Success Persons:	#1	#2
We both understand both the company's policies and the unwritten rules in the corporate culture about what is acceptable.		
We continue to do an excellent job, so no one can say that our work is deteriorating because of our relationship.		
We avoid meeting behind closed doors.		
We avoid touching and other forms of intimate contact in the workplace.		
We avoid the use of affectionate banter and cute nicknames during work hours.		
We get separate rooms when our jobs require that we travel together.		
Our positions are such that neither of us can be accused of career climbing by ''sleeping our way to the top.''		

Starting an office romance has its perils. In the early stages, expression of interest and affection can easily be misinterpreted and viewed as sexual harassment, particularly if the person who initiates it has a higher and therefore more powerful position. Men who have been taught that ''no'' means ''yes'' or ''maybe'' may also be in deep trouble if they press their case with a woman who is uncertain about what she wants. Women who dress or act seductively in order to get a man's attention run a similar risk.

T A S K 10

USE
RESOURCES

The task of creating a workplace in which both women and men work creatively and productively together has only begun. There is much more to learn. In the pages that follow you will find a listing of books, films and Consulting Services. Using them can help your organization and you to reach your full potential.

THE COMMUNITY ROUNDTABLE

By working your way through this book, you are bringing about a new workplace in which the contributions and needs of both women and men are recognized and supported. It is a challenging and difficult job. But it can be done, particularly if people support each other with information and ideas.

For that reason, the authors and other experts who have helped to produce this book have formed a Community Roundtable, a forum for studying the issues, looking at opportunities, developing skills, and solving the problems of a diverse workforce.

You are invited to participate by sharing your experiences, ideas, and questions about how people with differences of gender, race, and culture can work better together. Use the space below to do this (add paper if necessary). Mail your thoughts to:

Community Roundtable
c/o Crisp Publications
1200 Hamilton Court
Menlo Park, CA 94025, USA

Name	**Title**
Organization	
Address	

RESOURCE GUIDE

A listing of books, articles, consultants and trainers as well as other products and services available to individuals and organizations who wish to continue to acquire more information and skills for managing gender diversity.

1. KNOW THE ISSUES

Kanter, Rosabeth Moss, with Barry A. Stein, *A Tale of "O": On being different in an organization.* Harper & Row, NY, $4.95 (Now out of print, but available in many libraries.)

LeClere, William, *Chaos, Organizations and the Future,* LMA, Inc., P.O. Box 140, Milford, NH 03055. 1989, Paper, $10.00 postpaid. This study by a colleague of the authors of *Men and Women: Partners at Work* shows how future trends in technology and society will affect people in the workplace. Bill conducts assessment workshops which help individuals discover the skills they need to be successful in the organization of the future.

LMA Inc. 365 Melendy Road, Milford, NH 03055, whose mission is "bringing organizations into the future" provides diversity consulting and training interventions, mini-workshops and keynote addresses, and other products and services for organizations who wish to "change the system" and manage gender and cultural diversity more effectively. A number of their programs are listed below. Call them at 603-672-0355.

ODT Inc., is a source of training programs on cultural and gender diversity. A free list of program topics is available by writing to P.O. Box 134, Amherst, MA 01004 (413) 549-1293. Several of their publications are listed below.

The Women and Men of Mountaintop Ventures, *Partners in Chaos.* Mountaintop Ventures, Inc., 1988. 280 Central Ave., Hartsvale NY, 10530.

RESOURCE GUIDE (Continued)

2. LEARN HOW PEOPLE & ORGANIZATIONS DEVELOP

De Wal Learning Design, 129 Parkside Drive, Toronto, Ontario M6R 2Y8 Canada. ''Global Nomad'' Merle de Wal provides the benefit of fifteen years corporate experience to organizations interested in interpersonal programs that address the needs of a multi-cultural workforce.

Pierce, Carol, *The Stages of Awareness for Women and Men Moving Away from Role Stereotyping,* New Dynamics, 21 Shore Drive, Laconia, NH 03246, 1986. (603) 524-1441. $7.00, 30 pages. A videotape on this topic is also available.

and Bill Page, *Male/Female Continuum: Paths to Colleagueship.* New Dynamics. 1988, $9.95, 42 pages with fold out chart.

Managing the Organizational Tightrope is a 3 day training program which gives participants the tools to diagnose their organization's culture and find the leverage points for change. From LMA, Inc.

3. ACCEPT GENDER DIFFERENCES

Dowling, Colette, *The Cinderella Complex: Women's Hidden Fear of Independence,* 1988, NY, Pocket Books, ISBN 0-671-640-75-5, 288 pages. Paper $4.95

Eisler, Riane, *The Chalice and the Blade: Our History, Our Future.* Harper & Row, San Francisco (Perennial Library) 1987, ISBN 0-06-250287-5. Hardcover $16.95

Epstein, Cynthia Fuchs, *Deceptive Distinctions: Sex, Gender and the Social Order.* 1988, New Haven, Yale University Press, ISBN 0-300-04175-6. Hardcover $25.00.

Farrell, Warren, *Why Men Are The Way They Are.* McGraw-Hill, NY. 1986, 404 pages. ISBN 0-07-019974-4 Hardcover $17.95.

Gilligan, Carol, *In a Different Voice: Psychological Theory and Woman's Development.* Harvard University Press, Cambridge, 1982. ISBN 0-674-54832-9, 192 pages. Paper, $6.95

Schaef, Anne Wilson, *Women's Reality: An Emerging Female System in the White Male Society.* Winston Press, 403 Oak Grove, Minneapolis, MN 55403. 1981, (612) 871-7000 ISBN 0-86683-753-1, 169 pages. Paper $7.95

Simons, George F., *Working Together,* Crisp Publications, Menlo Park, CA, 1989. ISBN 0-931961-85-8, 76 pages. Paper $8.95.

_____ ''The Ultimate Cultural Difference,'' reprint from the *International Review of Management—1988.* Available from ODT Inc.

Palos, Piedras, y Estereotipos (Sticks, Stones and Stereotypes) Available from: The Equity Institute, 48 North Pleasant, Amherst, MA 01002. (413) 256-0271

Valuing Diversity (3 films)
Part 1—''**Managing Differences''** (For managers, on how to get the best performance in the multicultural workplace).
Part 2—''**Diversity at Work''** (For employees, on how to succeed in a multicultural workforce).
Part 3—''**Communicating across Cultures''** (Twelve common communication problems resulting from cultural differences).
Available from: Copeland Griggs Productions, 302 23rd Ave., San Francisco, CA 94121. (415) 668-4200

4. SPEAK WITH RESPECT

Hill, Alette Olin, *Mother Tongue, Father Time: A Decade of Linguistic Revolt.* Indiana University Press, Bloomington, IN. 1986, ISBN 0-253-20389-9, 160 pages. $9.95.

Lakoff, Robin, *Language and Women's Place,* Harper and Row 1975, Paper $6.95 ISBN 0-06-090-389-4, 160 pages. Paper $7.95.

Spender, Dale, *Man Made Language,* Routledge & Kegan Paul, Ltd., 9 Park Street, Boston, MA 02108, 1980

RESOURCE GUIDE (Continued)

Judith C. Tingley, PhD, 727 E. Bethany Home Road, Suite C-102, Phoenix, AZ 85014, 602-264-6662, speaks and leads seminars on the subject of Male-Female Communication and edits a quarterly newsletter, ''The Communicator.''

5. LEARN FROM EACH OTHER

Bools, Barbara & Lydia Swan, *Power Failure.* St. Martins, New York. 1989, ISBN 0-312-02632-3 $16.95.

Cohen, Sherry Suib, *Tender Power: A Revolutionary Approach to Work and Intimacy,* 1988, NY, Addison-Wesley, ISBN 0-201-09242-5. Hardcover $15.95.

Harragan, Betty Lehan, *Games Mother Never Taught You.* Warner Books, New York. 1977, ISBN 0-446-3400-1, 400 pages. Paper $4.95.

Sargent, Alice, *The Adrogynous Manager,* NY, 1983, AMACOM Books, ISBN 0-8144-7601-5, 192 pages. Paper $8.95.

6. CREATE UNDERSTANDING

Bone, Diane, *The Business of Listening,* Crisp Publications, Menlo Park, CA 1988, ISBN 0-931961-34-3, 80 pages. Paper $8.95.

Organizational Systems, Associates, 591 Brigham St., Marlboro, MA 01752, 508-481-8343, under the direction of Walter LeFlore provides seminars and instruction for understanding and dealing with situations where gender and racial differences are critical.

Positive Power and Influence is a 4 day training program which develops the skills to hear others and to be heard by them through a range of flexible communication styles. Available from LMA Inc.

7. CREATE AGREEMENTS

Maddux, Robert B., *Successful Negotiation,* Crisp Publications, Menlo Park, CA. 1989, ISBN 0-921961-09-2, 72 pages. Paper $8.95.

Positive Negotiation is a 4 day training program which focuses on creating agreement maintaining positive relationships in conflict situations. Available from LMA, Inc.

8. COLLABORATE

Baron, Alma S. and Ken Abrahamsen, ''Will He—or Won't He—Work with a Female Manager?'' in **Management Review,** November, 1981, AMACOM Publications.

Bern, Dr. Paula, *How to Work for a Woman Boss: Even if You'd Rather Not,* 1987, NY, Dodd, Mead & Company, Inc., ISBN 0-396-08839-2, 207 pages. Hardcover $15.95. Also available from ODT Inc.

Briles, Judith, *Woman to Woman: from Sabotage to Support,* 1987, Fair Hills, NJ, New Horizon Press, ISBN 0-88282-032-X, Hardcover $17.95. 298 pages.

Chapman, Elwood, N., *Winning at Human Relations,* Crisp Publications, Menlo Park, CA. 1988, ISBN 0-931961-86-6, $8.95. 80 pages.

Creating Collaboration is a 3 day training program which provides participants with the tools to gain commitment and motivate others to make and implement decisions. Available from LMA, Inc.

''Gender Hostility,'' Audiotape, worksheets and facilitators guide. From ODT Inc. $35.00.

Josefowitz, Natasha, PhD, ''How to Deal with a Sexist Boss,'' a tip sheet from ODT Inc. $2.00.

John McPherson, Organization transformation consultant and trainer, works with issues of gender and race within business organizations of all sizes. Valuing differences continues to be the foundation of his positive approach to helping employees, managers and organizations become the best they can be. For more information, call John at 617-545-5751.

Monica Armour, P.O. Box 676, Toronto, ONT M5S 2Y4, Canada, is a leader in the field of diversity, offering customized consulting and consulting to both public and private organizations.

9. PAY ATTENTION TO EACH OTHER

Maniero, Lisa, *Office Romance: Love, Sex and Power in the Workplace.* Rawson Associates. 1989, ISBN 0-99256-34-1. Hardcover $17.95.

Nunes, Marianna, ''The Art of Flirting,'' audiotape, $10.00 postpaid from her at 1746 Leavenworth Street, San Francisco, CA 94109, 415-673-6775. Marianna teaches courses in flirting and self-esteem for organizations and the public.

Risser, Rita, *How to Work With Men: The Rita Method for Working Women.* Rita Risser, 803 Pine Street, Santa Cruz, CA 1984, (408) 244-9993 x104   64 pages. $12.00. Rita also conducts programs for organizations on ''Managing within the Law,'' addressing such issues as equal opportunity and harassment from a legal point of view.